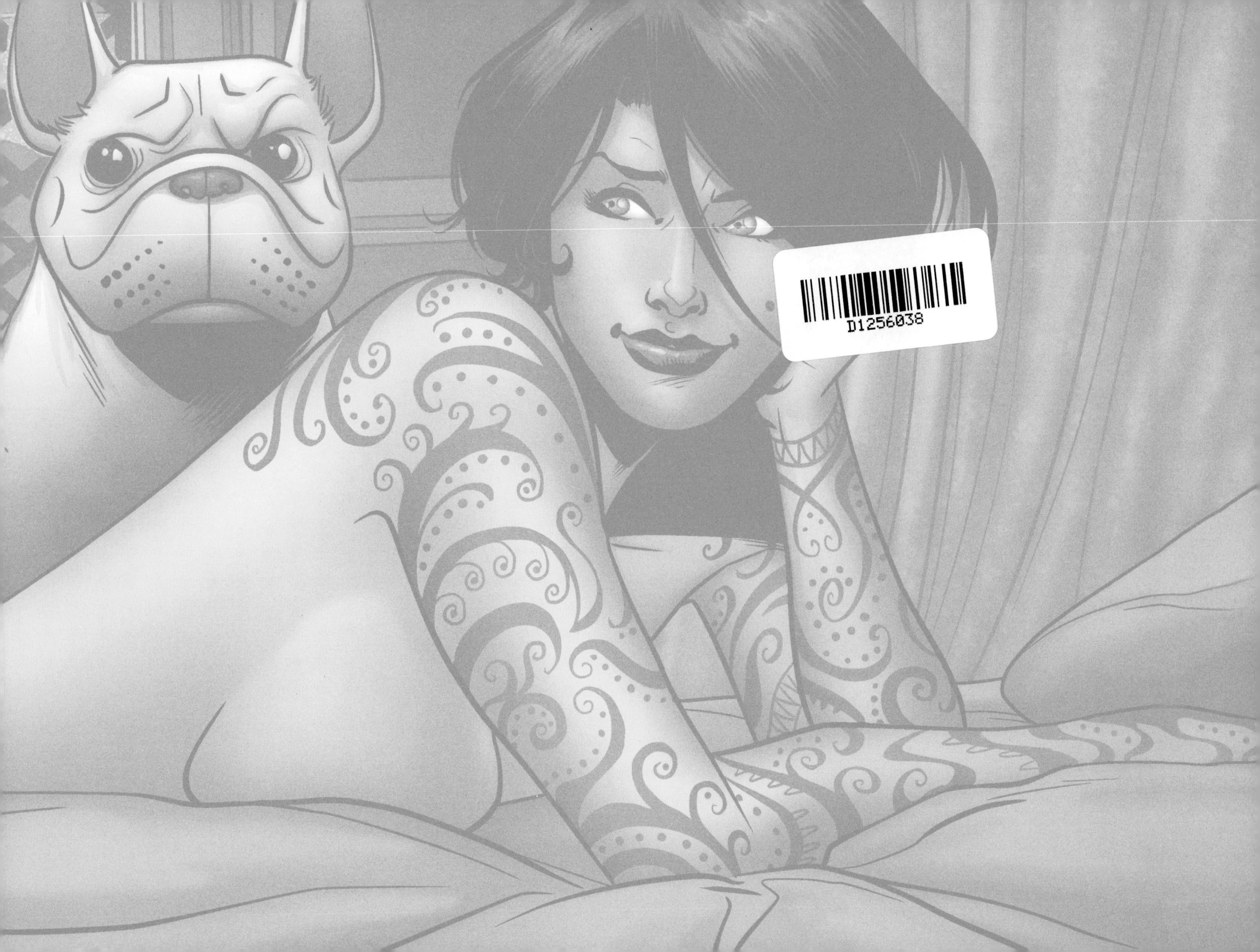

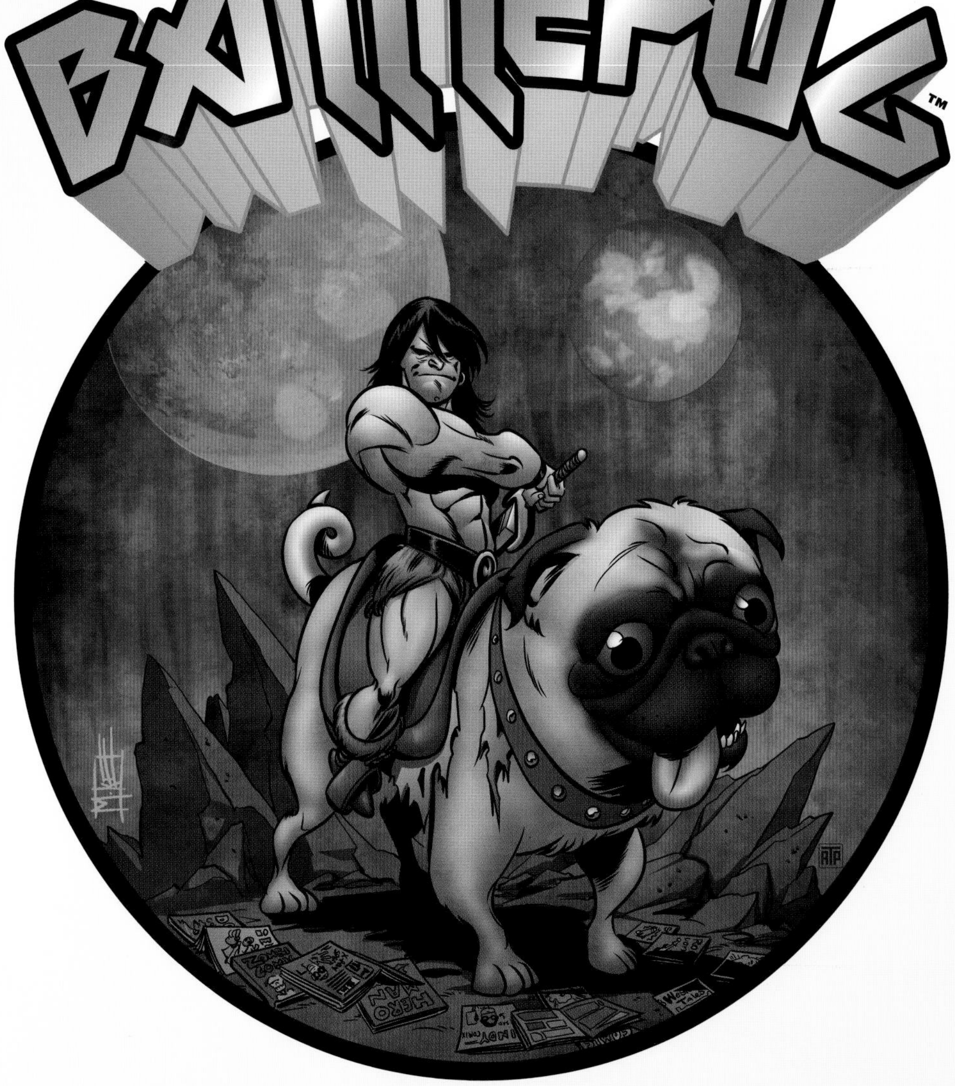
BATTLEPUG™

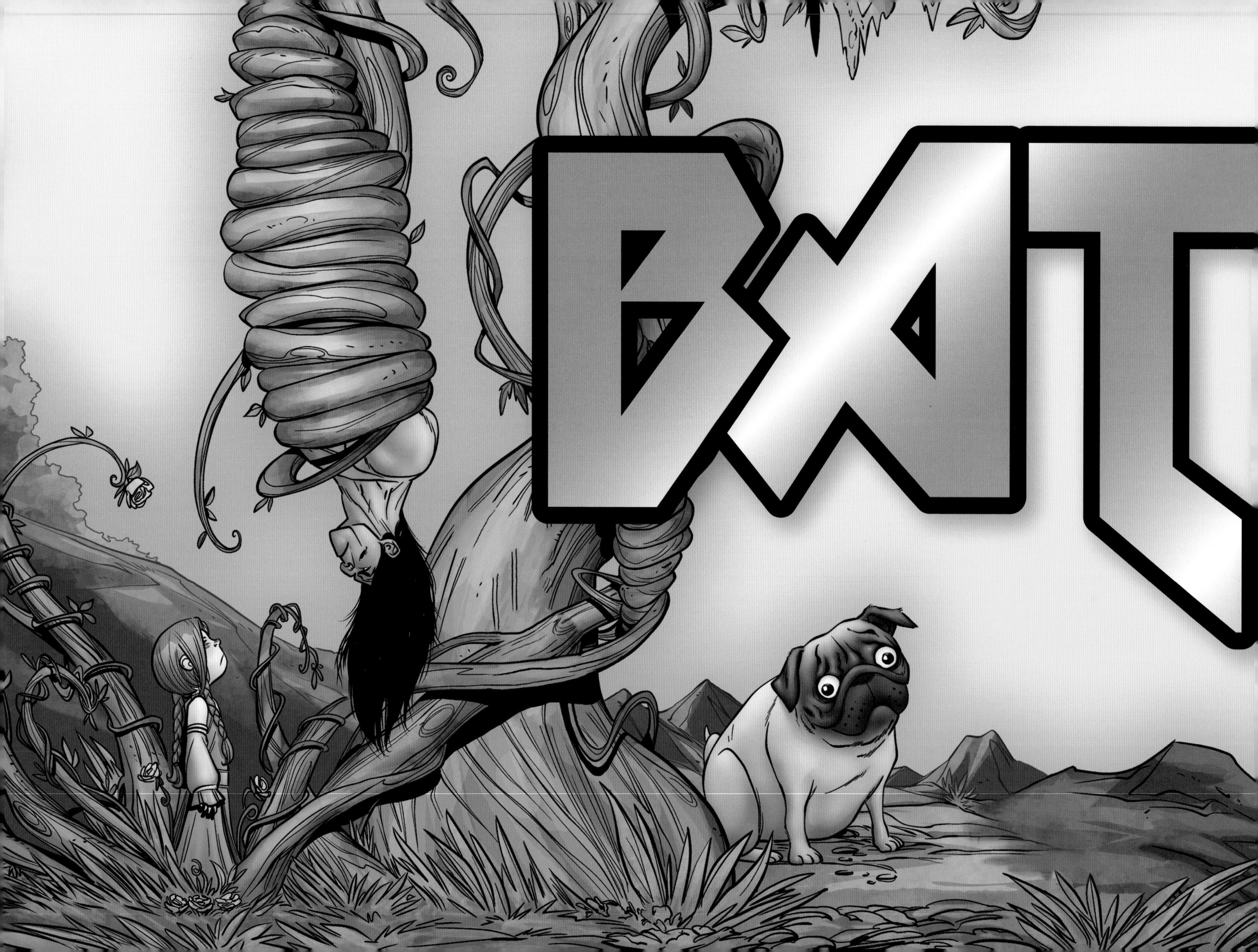

VOLUME 2: THIS SAVAGE BONE

Writer and Artist
MIKE NORTON

Color Artist
ALLEN PASSALAQUA

Letterer
CHRIS CRANK

Cover Artists
MIKE NORTON AND
DOMINIC MARCO

DARK HORSE
BOOKS

Publisher	Editor	Assistant Editor	Designer	Digital Art and Production
MIKE RICHARDSON	**PATRICK THORPE**	**EVERETT PATTERSON**	**TINA ALESSI**	**CHRISTIANNE GOUDREAU**

Special thanks to Brion Salazar, Josh Emmons, and iFanboy.

Published by Dark Horse Books, a division of Dark Horse Comics, Inc.
10956 SE Main Street, Milwaukie, Oregon 97222
DarkHorse.com

To find a comic shop in your area, call the Comic Shop Locator Service: (888) 266-4226

First edition: August 2013
ISBN 978-1-61655-201-5
10 9 8 7 6 5 4 3 2 1

Printed in China

MIKE RICHARDSON President and Publisher NEIL HANKERSON Executive Vice President TOM WEDDLE Chief Financial Officer RANDY STRADLEY Vice President of Publishing MICHAEL MARTENS Vice President of Book Trade Sales ANITA NELSON Vice President of Business Affairs SCOTT ALLIE Editor in Chief MATT PARKINSON Vice President of Marketing DAVID SCROGGY Vice President of Product Development DALE LAFOUNTAIN Vice President of Information Technology DARLENE VOGEL Senior Director of Print, Design, and Production KEN LIZZI General Counsel DAVEY ESTRADA Editorial Director CHRIS WARNER Senior Books Editor DIANA SCHUTZ Executive Editor CARY GRAZZINI Director of Print and Development LIA RIBACCHI Art Director CARA NIECE Director of Scheduling TIM WIESCH Director of International Licensing MARK BERNARDI Director of Digital Publishing

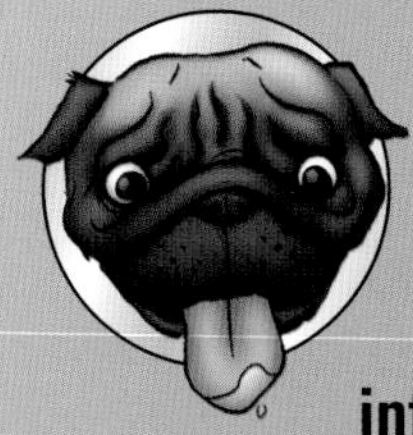

INTRODUCTION

MIKE NORTON . . . FELLOW TENNESSEAN. MAN AMONG MEN. BIG HAIRY DUDE.

I first met Mike Norton years ago when he moved to Nashville from Memphis. It was at the time his infamous gangster-rap duo, the Five White Guys Quartet, had just been run out of town during the notorious Memorial Day Memphis Rap Battle and BBQ Competition. If the nation learned anything that sacred holiday weekend, it was that even in a rap battle . . . it's never okay for white guys to use the N-word, and you never, NEVER boil ribs.

Mike, the only survivor of the Five White Guys Quartet, was trying to lie low. But for a man the size of Mike Norton, that's a hard thing to do. In order to survive, he threw away all ties to the seedy yet lucrative life of white gangster rap and immersed himself in the less than masculine world of comic books. His plan worked. Submerged amongst the bent spines, bad eyes, and timid demeanor of unwashed comicdom, no one suspected that the albino Sasquatch equivalent of the Notorious B.I.G. was hidden in Nashville.

So a bunch of crap happened after that, mostly involving Snoop and al-Qaeda. Clack-Clack! Bang-Bang! Not worth mentioning really. Anyhoo, Norton started trying to draw comic books. He really sucked at it. His nature was rap battling, not funny-book making. To hear him tell it, he realized that his music was misogynistic and degrading towards women and the handicapped and he ended up falling in love with the art form of sequential storytelling. But I know he sought the training of a secret monk cult in Brazil that specialized in the making of comic books about insects that crocheted intricate shower curtains to forget past heartbreaks. These crocheting-insect comics were renowned for their depth of artistic skill, impeccable layouts, and storytelling. Inking so subtle as to make John Denver weep if he had tear ducts or a soul. You may ask, "Why have I not heard of these magnificent works of art?!" I'll tell you why . . . Nobody wants to read whiny crocheting-insect comics! Lame! Pouting little antennae-wiggling lame asses! You really want to read 152 pages of a bug knitting and crying? Make you put a gun in your mouth, man. But monks are into that boring crap. It's because they got nothing better to do. They've deprived themselves of sex, and that'll make you go nutty.

Anyway, Mike Norton came out of Brazil wild eyed and half crazy. Praying to a shower curtain braided from human hair. But once he had some sex, he could draw like a champ!

Mike drew a bunch of superhero books for Marvel and DC then. Good stuff. But then fate stepped in. The moment Mike came up with his Eisner Award–winning webcomic, *Battlepug*, is now a legendary story. As the knowledgeable now tell, it was on Easter Sunday in a Thai food joint called the Uncomfortable Elephant. Mike, who is an excessive pug hoarder, was treating his gaggle of little monkey-faced dogs to some spicy fried pork

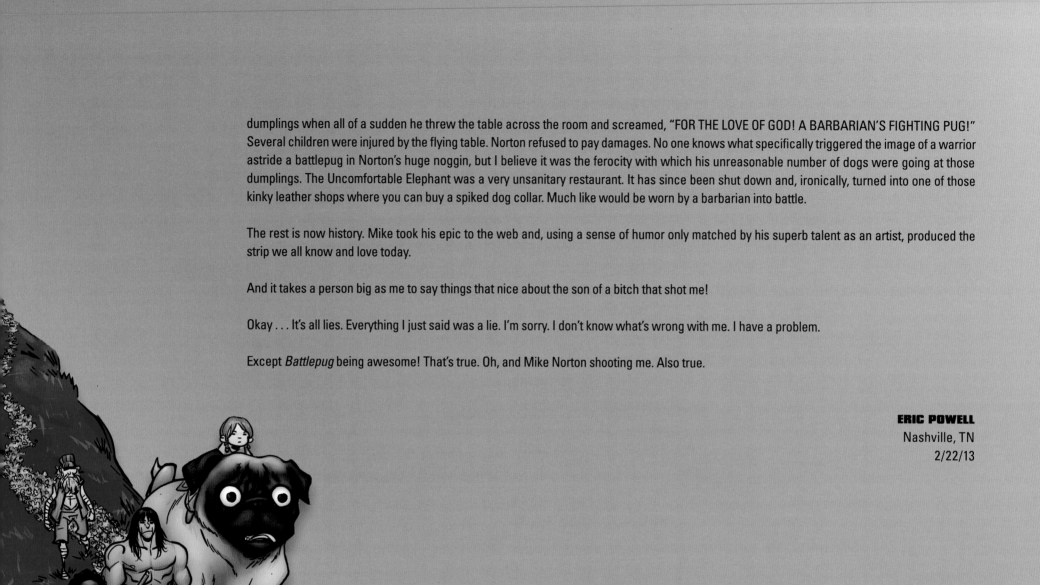

dumplings when all of a sudden he threw the table across the room and screamed, "FOR THE LOVE OF GOD! A BARBARIAN'S FIGHTING PUG!" Several children were injured by the flying table. Norton refused to pay damages. No one knows what specifically triggered the image of a warrior astride a battlepug in Norton's huge noggin, but I believe it was the ferocity with which his unreasonable number of dogs were going at those dumplings. The Uncomfortable Elephant was a very unsanitary restaurant. It has since been shut down and, ironically, turned into one of those kinky leather shops where you can buy a spiked dog collar. Much like would be worn by a barbarian into battle.

The rest is now history. Mike took his epic to the web and, using a sense of humor only matched by his superb talent as an artist, produced the strip we all know and love today.

And it takes a person big as me to say things that nice about the son of a bitch that shot me!

Okay . . . It's all lies. Everything I just said was a lie. I'm sorry. I don't know what's wrong with me. I have a problem.

Except *Battlepug* being awesome! That's true. Oh, and Mike Norton shooting me. Also true.

ERIC POWELL
Nashville, TN
2/22/13

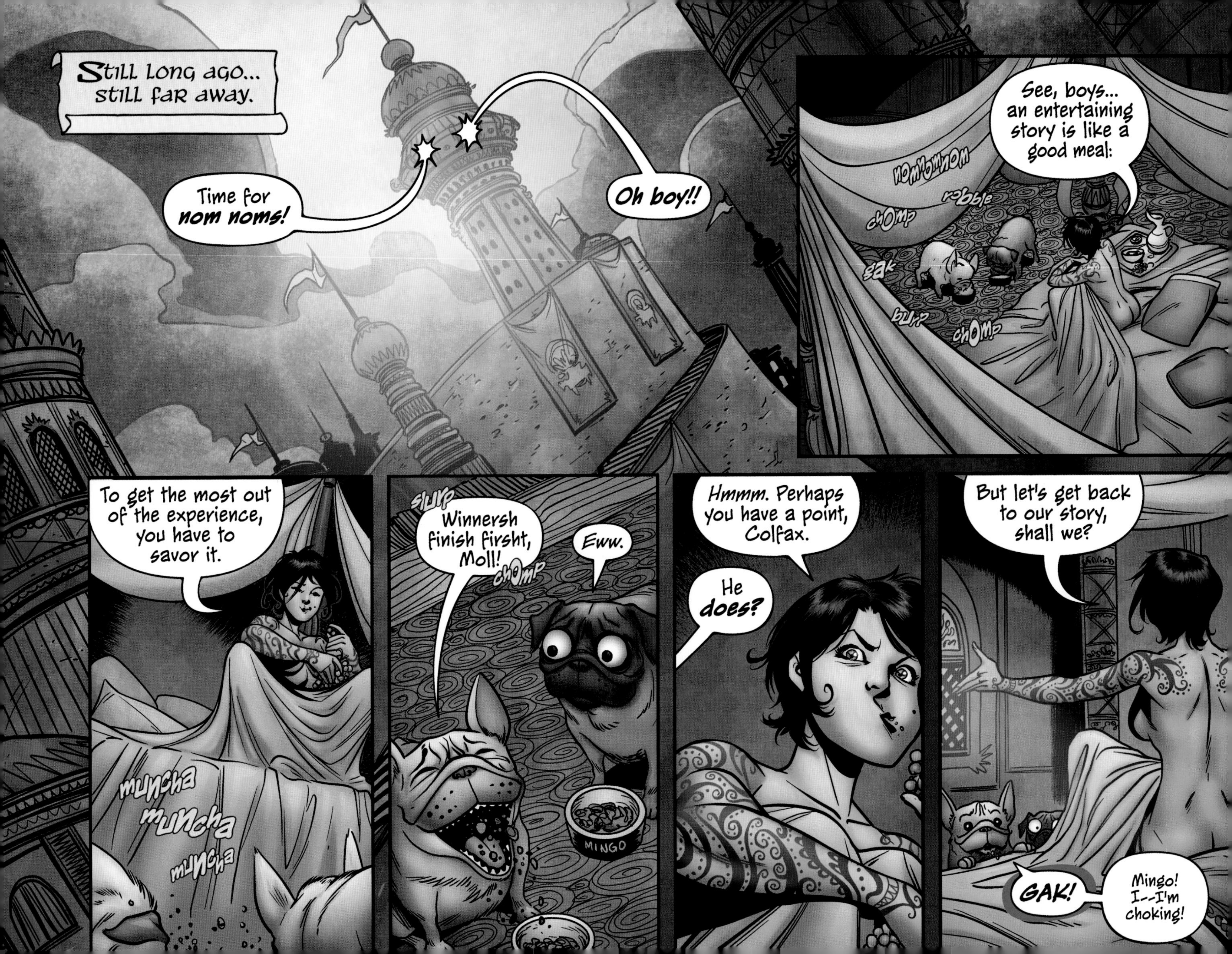
Still long ago... still far away.
Time for nom noms!
Oh boy!!
See, boys... an entertaining story is like a good meal:
nomnomnom
robble
chomp
gak
burp
chomp
To get the most out of the experience, you have to savor it.
muncha
muncha
muncha
slurp
Winnersh finish firsht, Moll!
chomp
Eww.
MINGO
Hmmm. Perhaps you have a point, Colfax.
He does?
But let's get back to our story, shall we?
GAK!
Mingo! I--I'm choking!

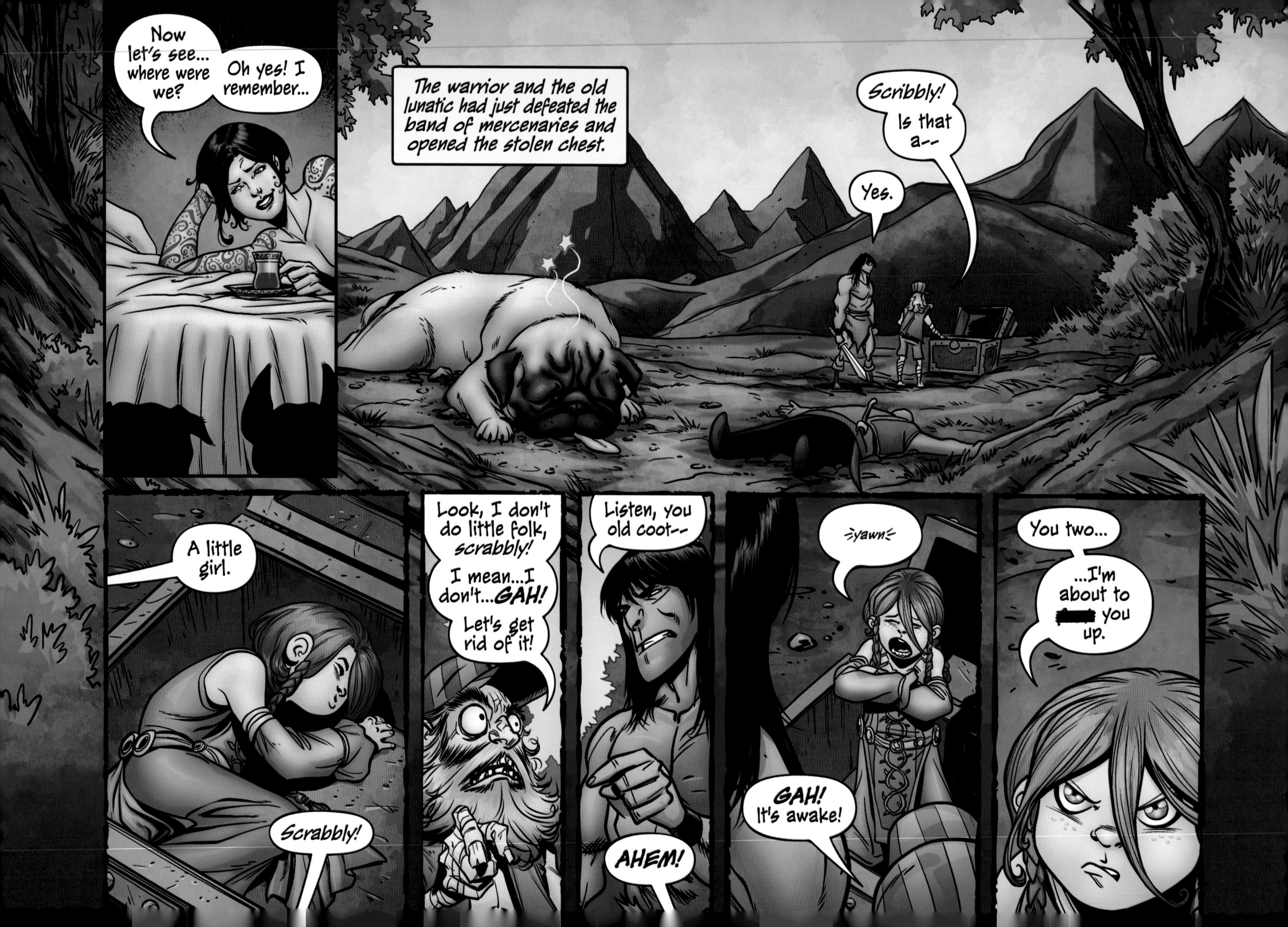

Now let's see... where were we?
Oh yes! I remember...
The warrior and the old lunatic had just defeated the band of mercenaries and opened the stolen chest.
Scribbly!
Is that a--
Yes.
A little girl.
Scrabbly!
Look, I don't do little folk, scrabbly!
I mean...I don't...GAH!
Let's get rid of it!
Listen, you old coot--
AHEM!
yawn
GAH! It's awake!
You two...
...I'm about to [redacted] you up.

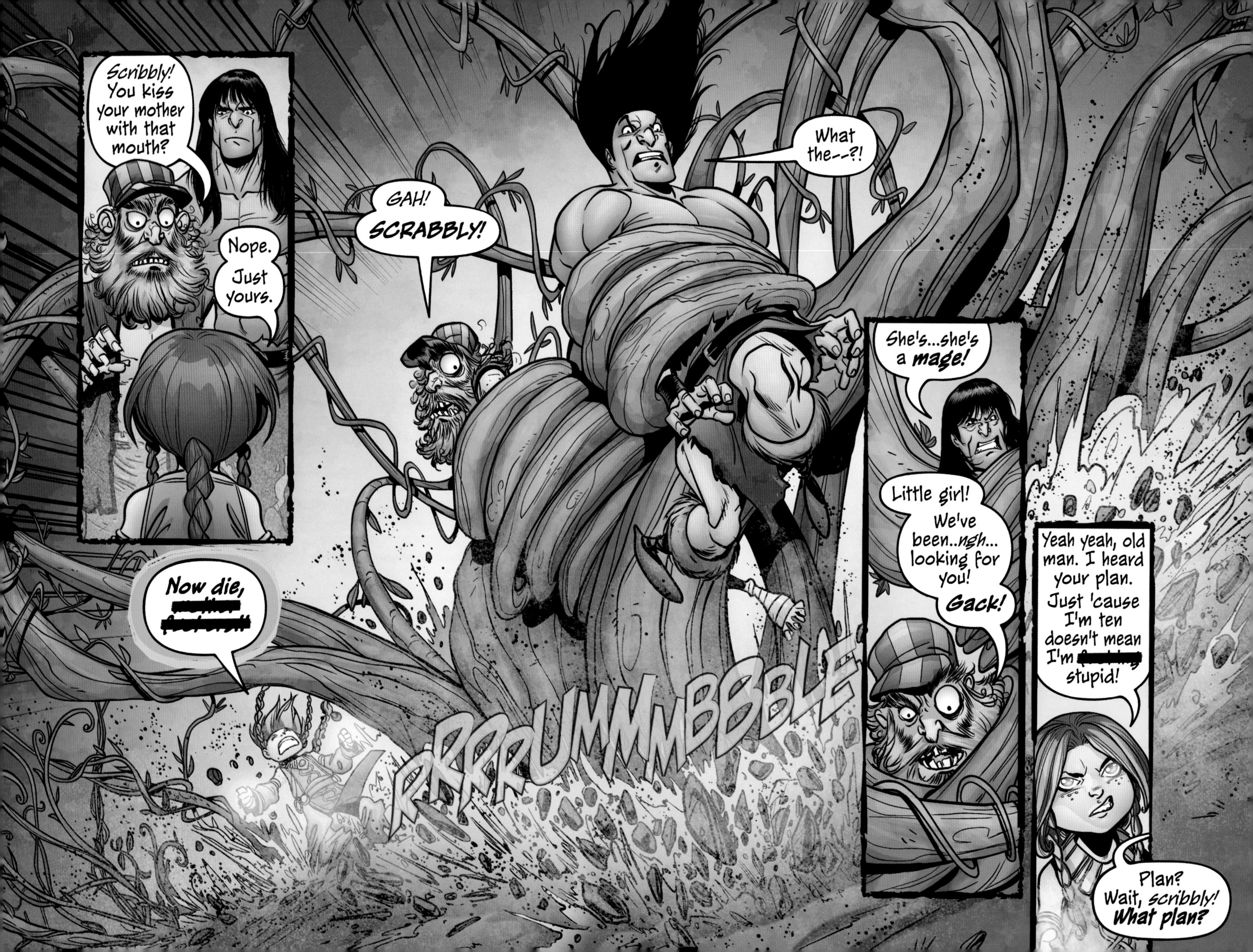
Scribbly! You kiss your mother with that mouth?
Nope. Just yours.
GAH! SCRABBLY!
What the--?!
Now die, [redacted]
RRRRUMMMMBBBBLE
She's...she's a mage!
Little girl! We've been..ngh... looking for you! Gack!
Yeah yeah, old man. I heard your plan. Just 'cause I'm ten doesn't mean I'm [redacted] stupid!
Plan? Wait, scribbly! What plan?

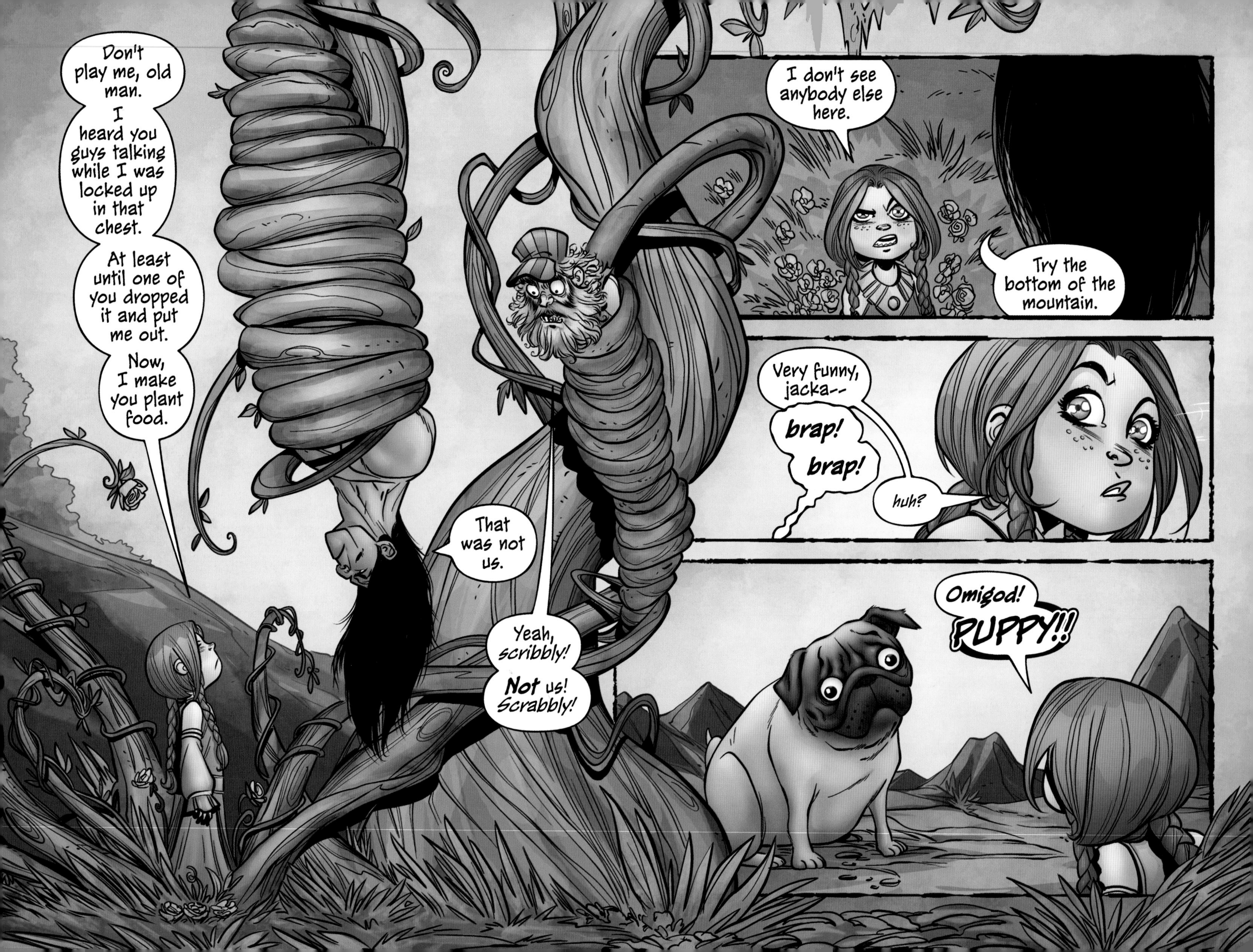
Don't play me, old man.
I heard you guys talking while I was locked up in that chest.
At least until one of you dropped it and put me out.
Now, I make you plant food.
That was not us.
Yeah, scribbly!
Not us! Scrabbly!
I don't see anybody else here.
Try the bottom of the mountain.
Very funny, jacka--
brap!
brap!
huh?
Omigod!
PUPPY!!

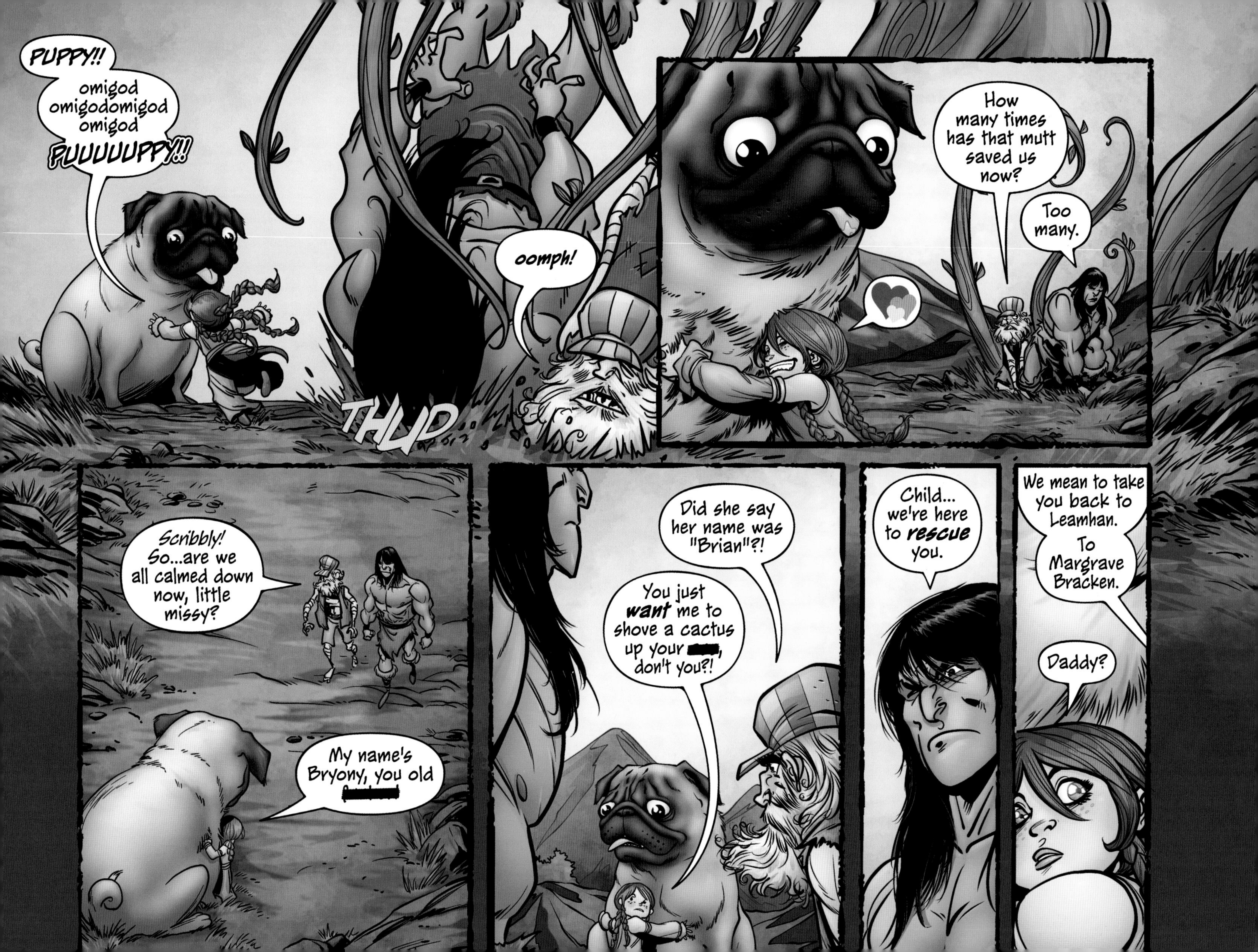
PUPPY!!
omigod omigodomigod omigod
PUUUUUPPY!!
THUD
oomph!
How many times has that mutt saved us now?
Too many.
Scribbly! So...are we all calmed down now, little missy?
My name's Bryony, you old [redacted]
Did she say her name was "Brian"?!
You just *want* me to shove a cactus up your [redacted], don't you?!
Child... we're here to **rescue** you.
We mean to take you back to Leamhan.
To Margrave Bracken.
Daddy?

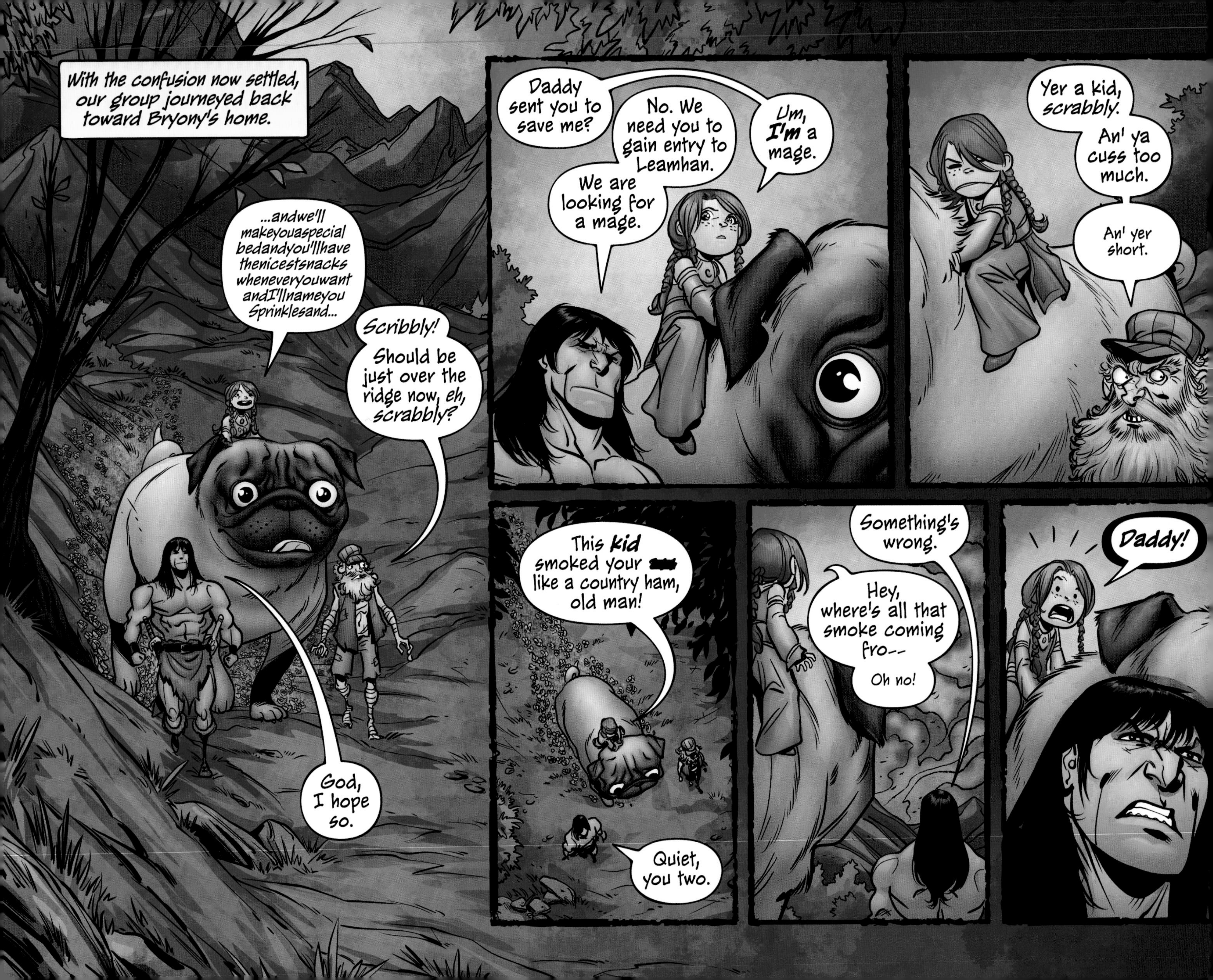

With the confusion now settled, our group journeyed back toward Bryony's home.
...andwe'll makeyouaspecial bedandyou'llhave thenicestsnacks wheneveryouwant andI'llnameyou Sprinklesand...
Scribbly!
Should be just over the ridge now, eh, scrabbly?
God, I hope so.
Daddy sent you to save me?
No. We need you to gain entry to Leamhan.
We are looking for a mage.
Um, *I'm* a mage.
Yer a kid, scrabbly.
An' ya cuss too much.
An' yer short.
This *kid* smoked your [redacted] like a country ham, old man!
Quiet, you two.
Something's wrong.
Hey, where's all that smoke coming fro--
Oh no!
Daddy!

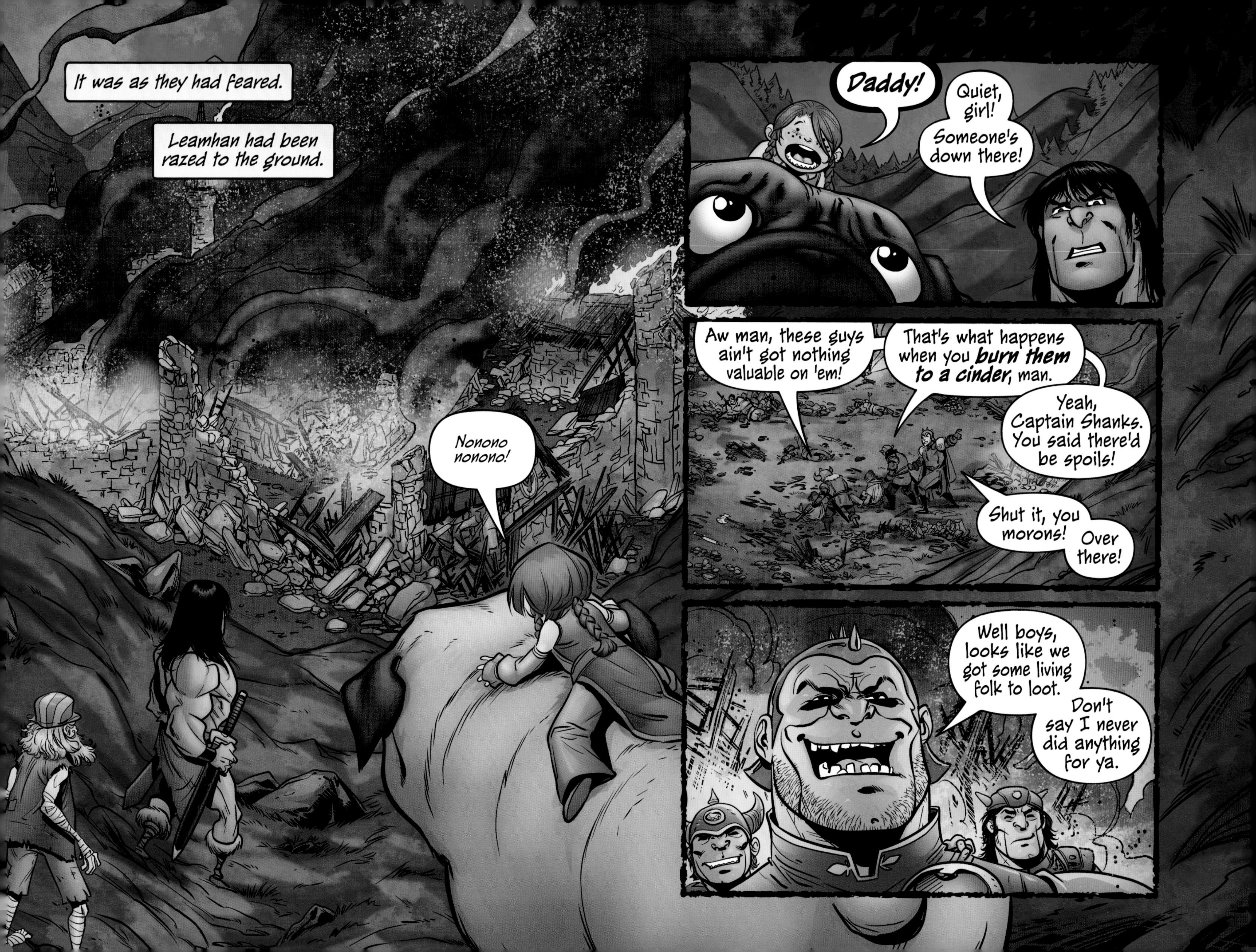
It was as they had feared.
Leamhan had been razed to the ground.
Nonono nonono!
Daddy!
Quiet, girl!
Someone's down there!
Aw man, these guys ain't got nothing valuable on 'em!
That's what happens when you **burn them to a cinder**, man.
Yeah, Captain Shanks. You said there'd be spoils!
Shut it, you morons!
Over there!
Well boys, looks like we got some living folk to loot.
Don't say I never did anything for ya.

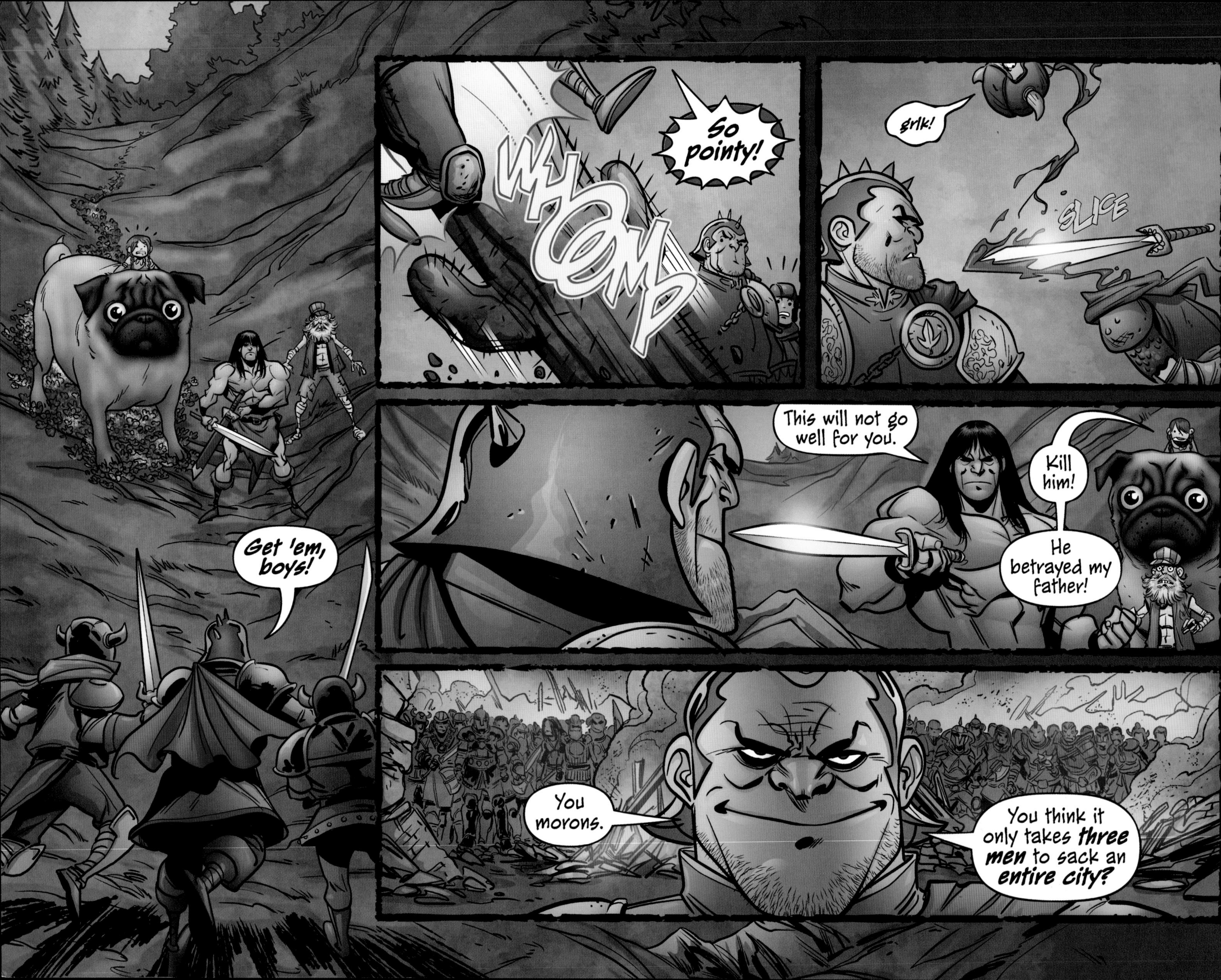
Get 'em, boys!
WHOMP
So pointy!
grlk!
SLICE
This will not go well for you.
Kill him!
He betrayed my father!
You morons.
You think it only takes **three men** to sack an ***entire city?***

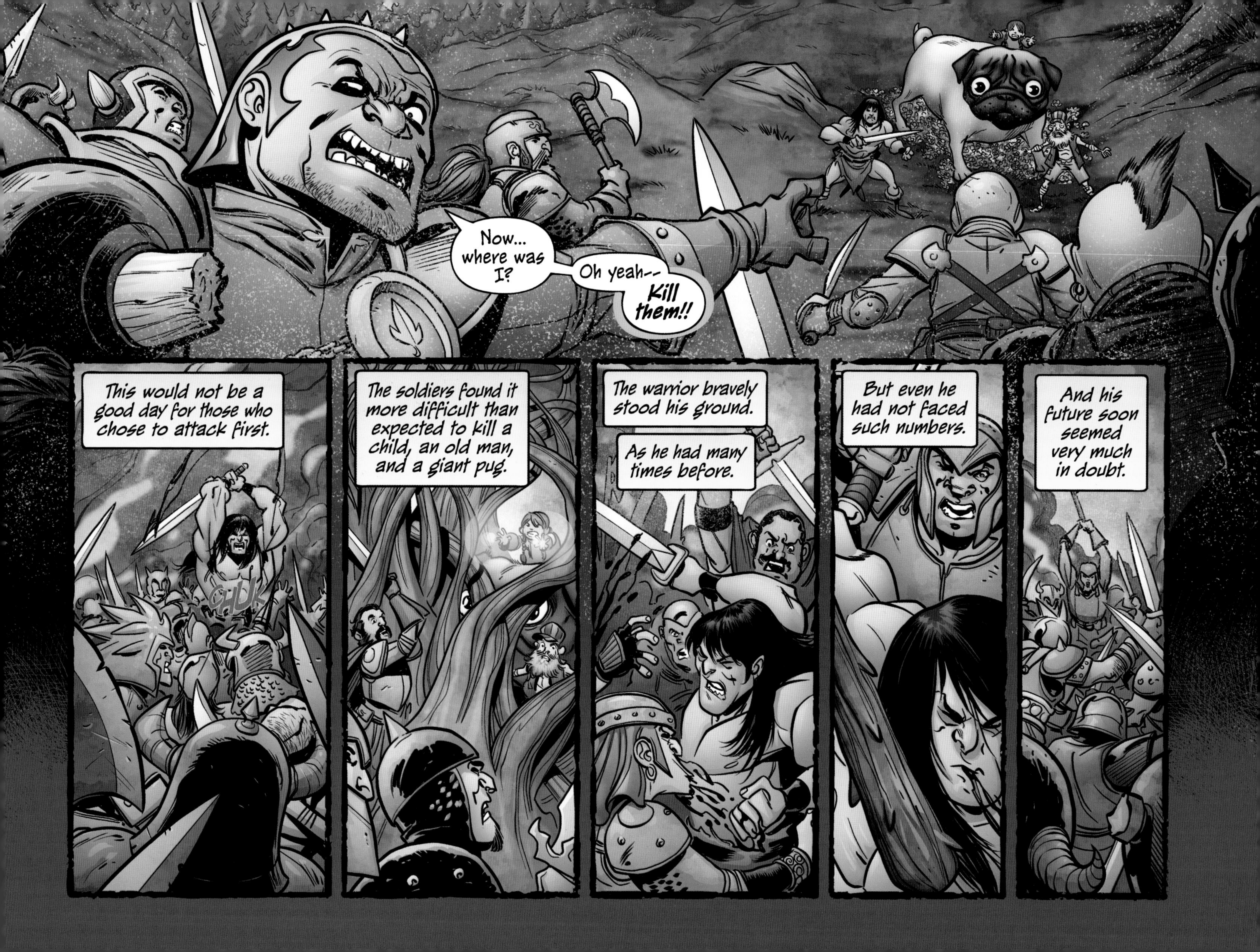
Now... where was I?
Oh yeah-- Kill them!!
This would not be a good day for those who chose to attack first.
CHUK
The soldiers found it more difficult than expected to kill a child, an old man, and a giant pug.
The warrior bravely stood his ground.
As he had many times before.
But even he had not faced such numbers.
And his future soon seemed very much in doubt.

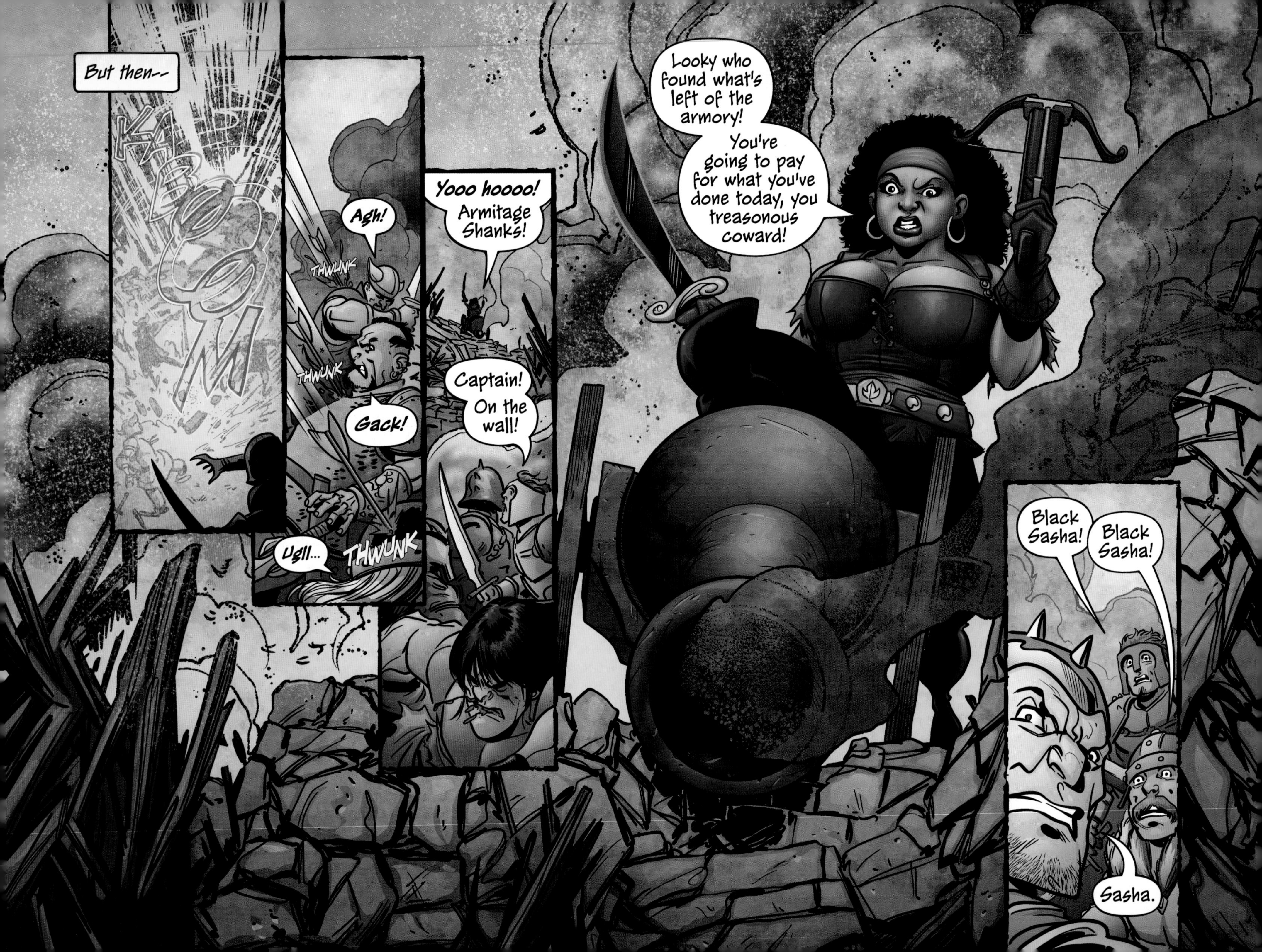
But then--
KABOOM
Agh!
THWUNK
THWUNK
Gack!
Ugll...
THWUNK
Yooo hoooo! Armitage Shanks!
Captain! On the wall!
Looky who found what's left of the armory!
You're going to pay for what you've done today, you treasonous coward!
Black Sasha!
Black Sasha!
Sasha.

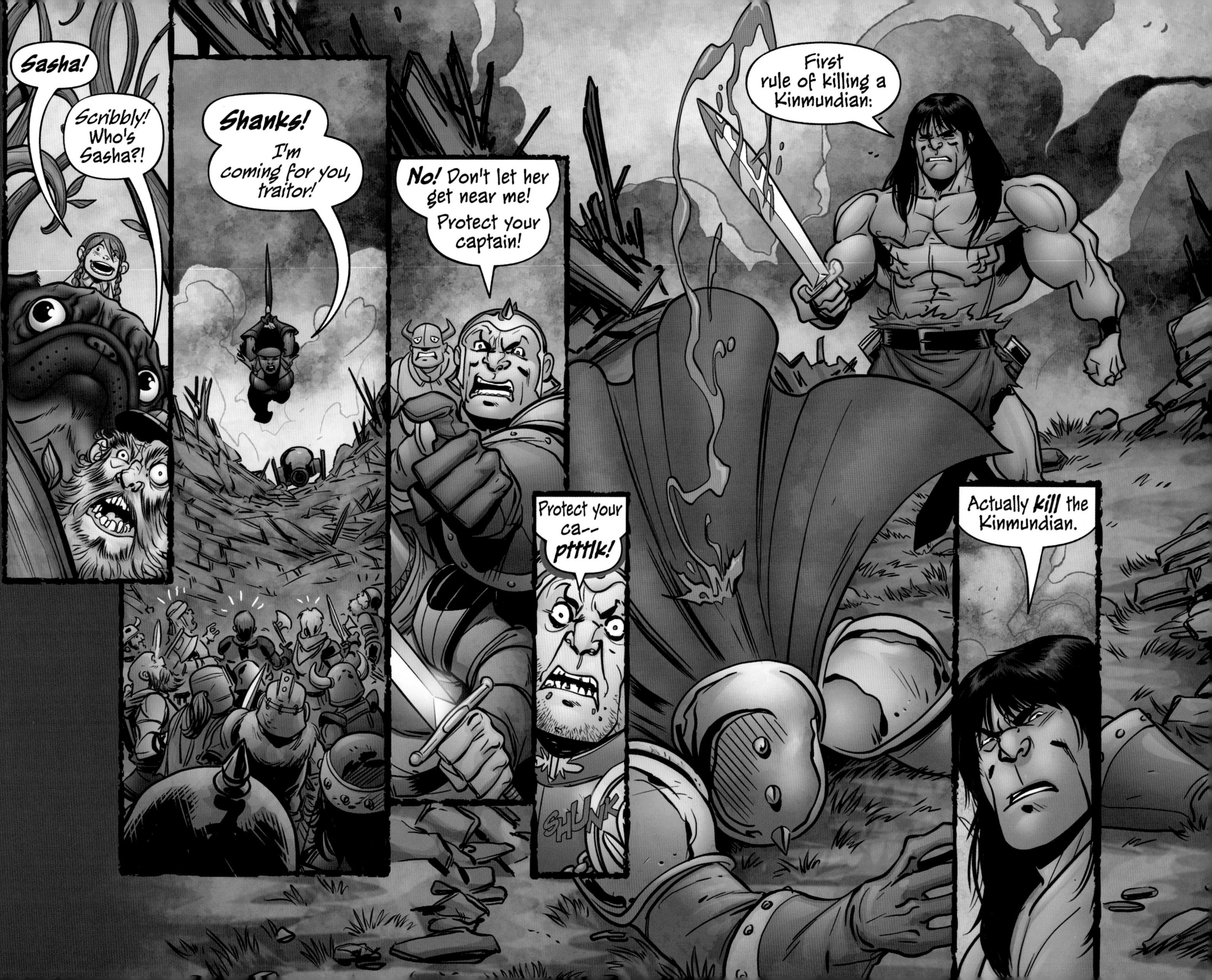
Sasha!
Scribbly! Who's Sasha?!
Shanks!
I'm coming for you, traitor!
No! Don't let her get near me!
Protect your captain!
Protect your ca-- pttt!k!
SHUNK
First rule of killing a Kinmundian:
Actually kill the Kinmundian.

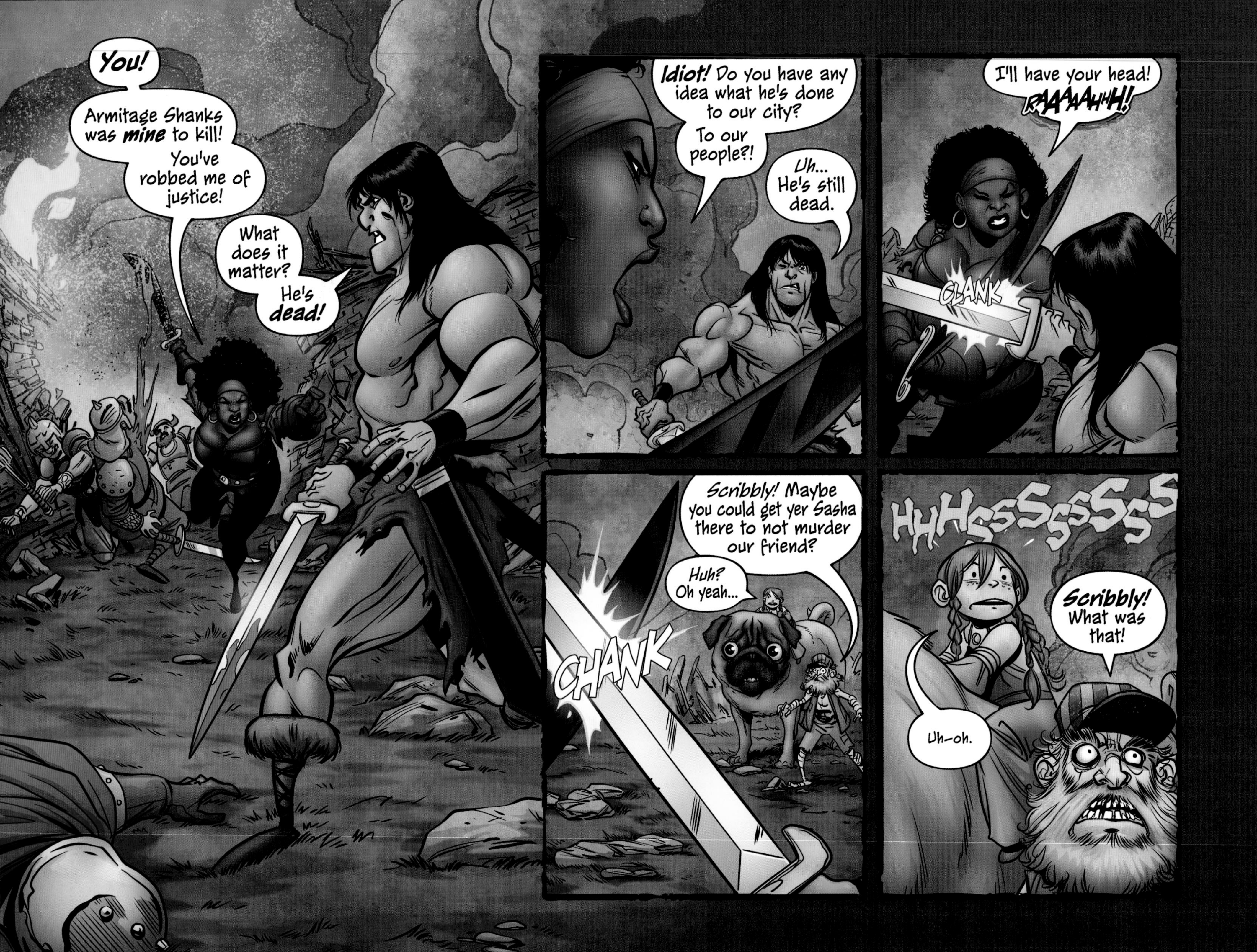
You!
Armitage Shanks was mine to kill!
You've robbed me of justice!
What does it matter?
He's dead!
Idiot! Do you have any idea what he's done to our city?
To our people?!
Uh... He's still dead.
I'll have your head!
RAAAAAHHH!
CLANK
Scribbly! Maybe you could get yer Sasha there to not murder our friend?
Huh? Oh yeah...
CHANK
HHHSSSSSSSS
Scribbly! What was that!
Uh-oh.

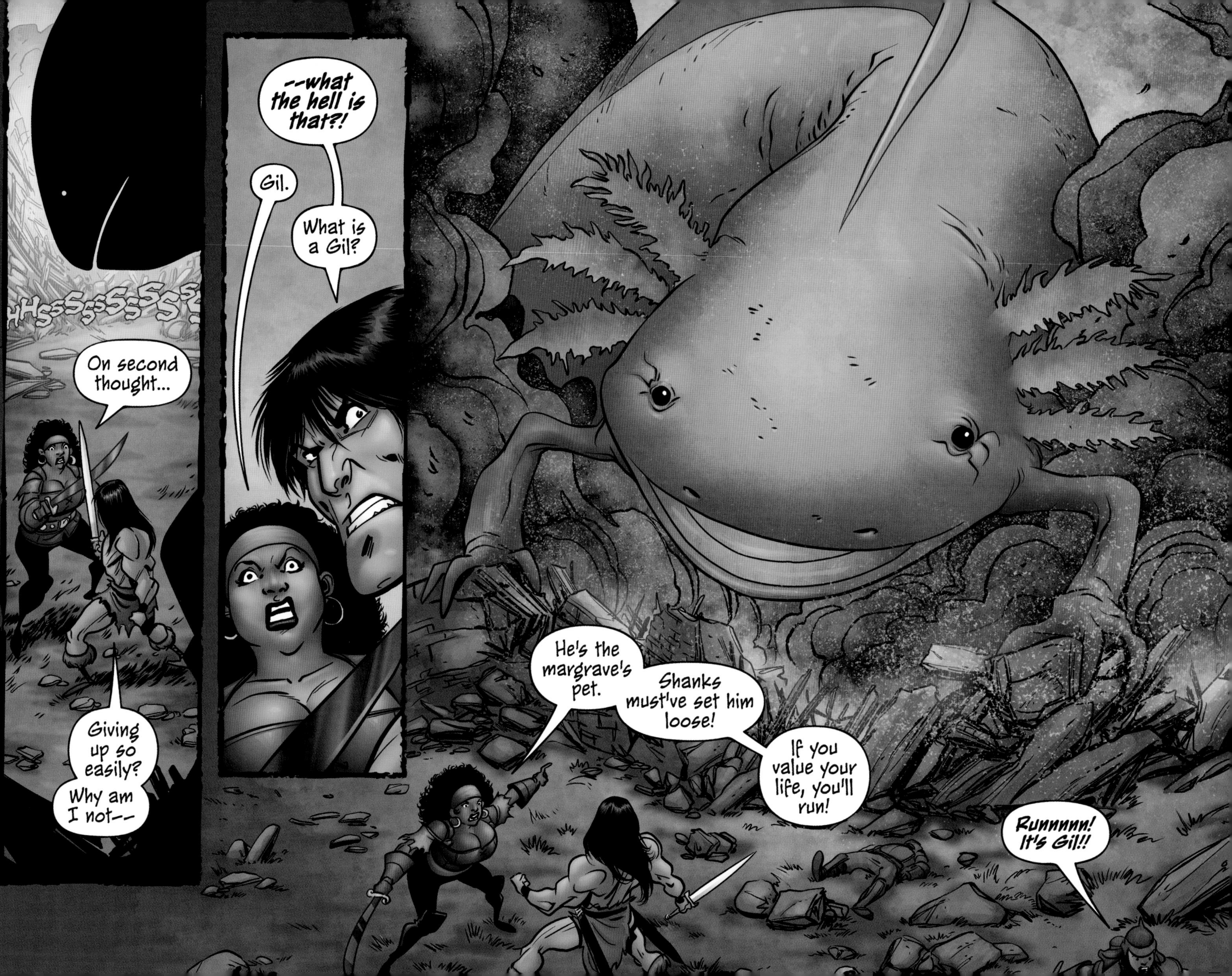
HSSSSSSSSS
On second thought...
Giving up so easily? Why am I not--
--what the hell is that?!
Gil.
What is a Gil?
He's the margrave's pet.
Shanks must've set him loose!
If you value your life, you'll run!
Runnnnn! It's Gil!!

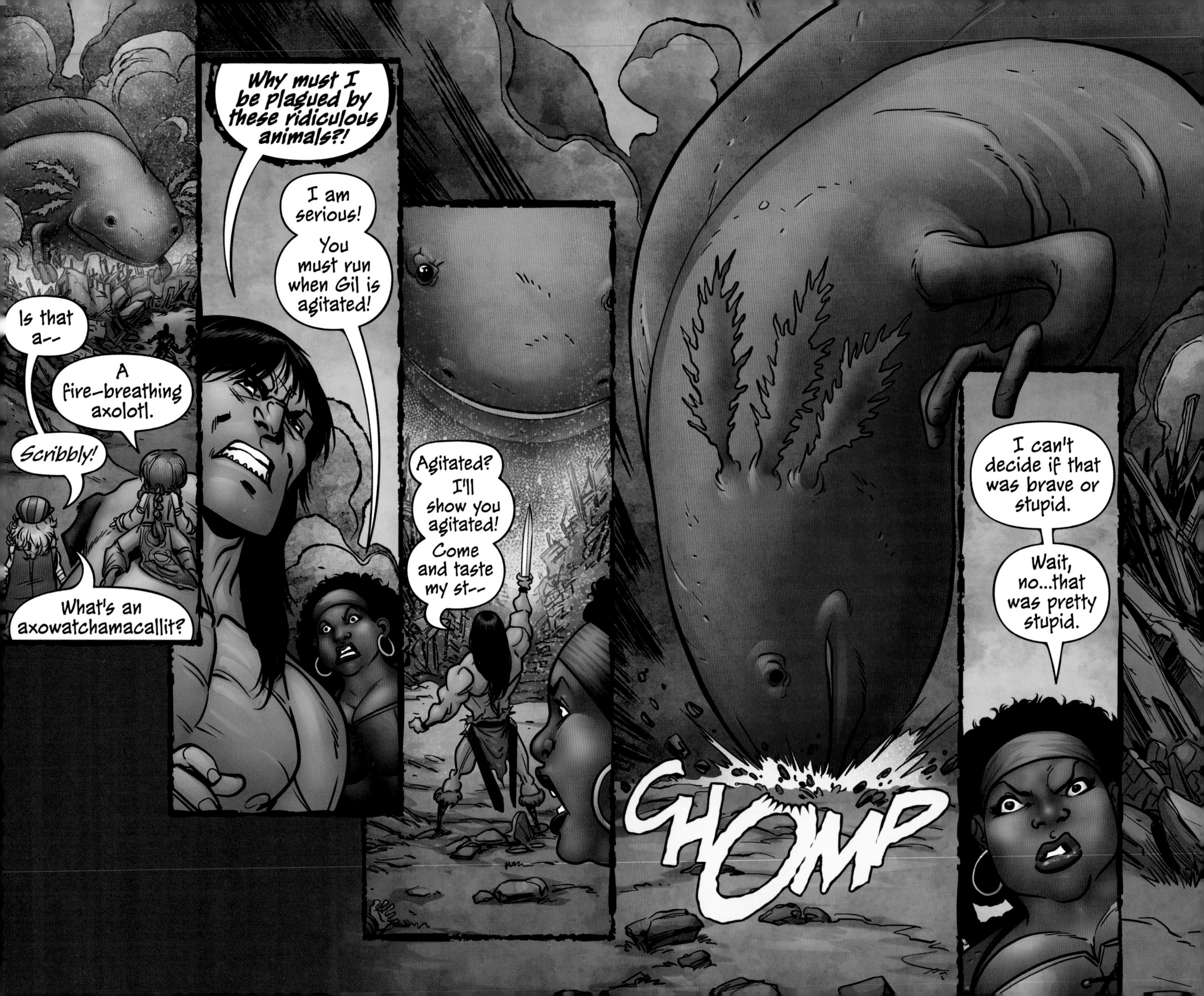
Is that a--
A fire-breathing axolotl.
Scribbly!
What's an axowatchamacallit?
Why must I be plagued by these ridiculous animals?!
I am serious!
You must run when Gil is agitated!
Agitated? I'll show you agitated!
Come and taste my st--
CHOMP
I can't decide if that was brave or stupid.
Wait, no...that was pretty stupid.

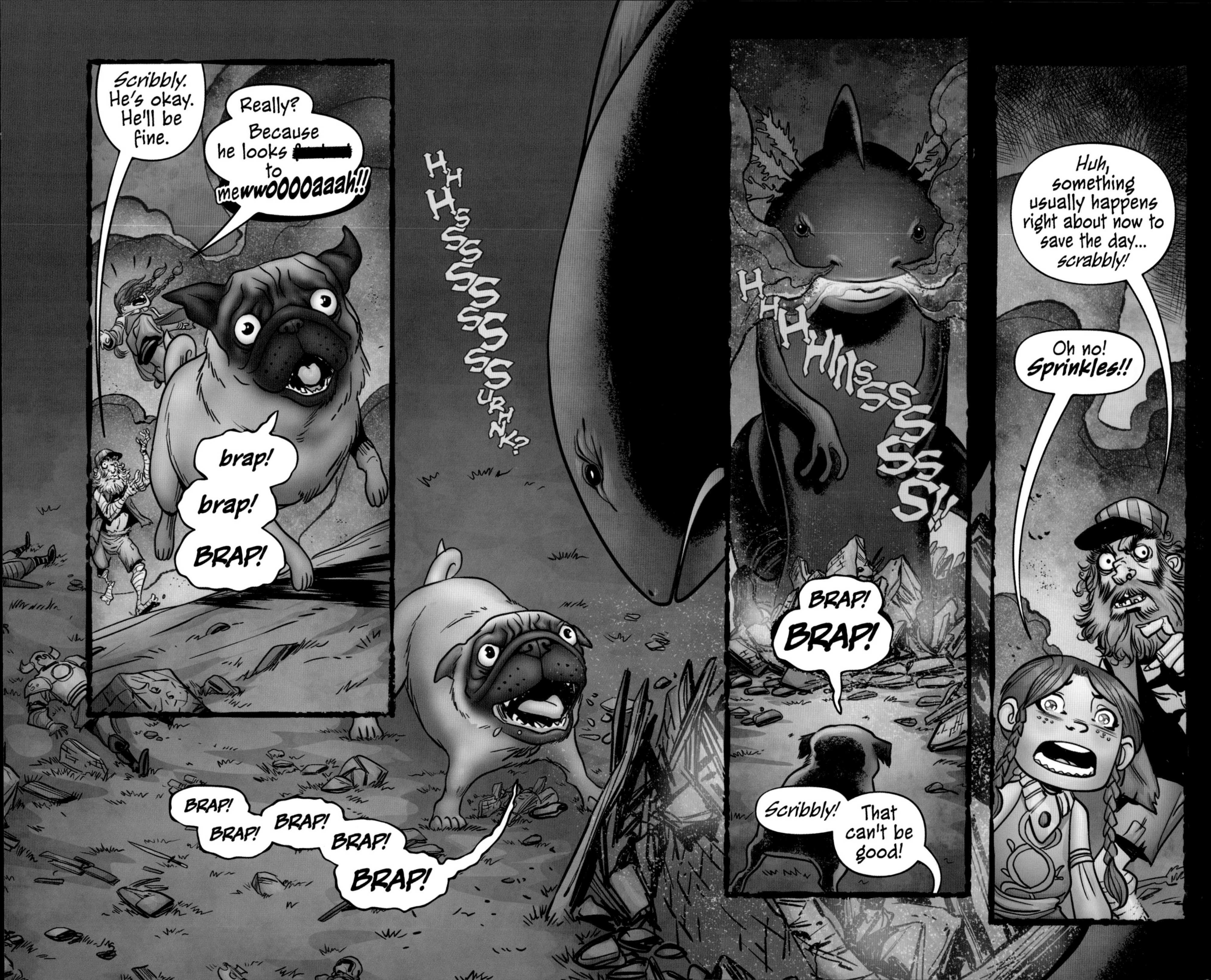

Scribbly. He's okay. He'll be fine.
Really? Because he looks [redacted] to mewwOOOOaaah!!
brap!
brap!
BRAP!
HHHSSSSSSSSSURHNK?
BRAP!
BRAP!
BRAP!
BRAP!
BRAP!
HHHHHSSSSSSSS!!
BRAP!
BRAP!
Scribbly!
That can't be good!
Huh, something usually happens right about now to save the day... scrabbly!
Oh no! Sprinkles!!

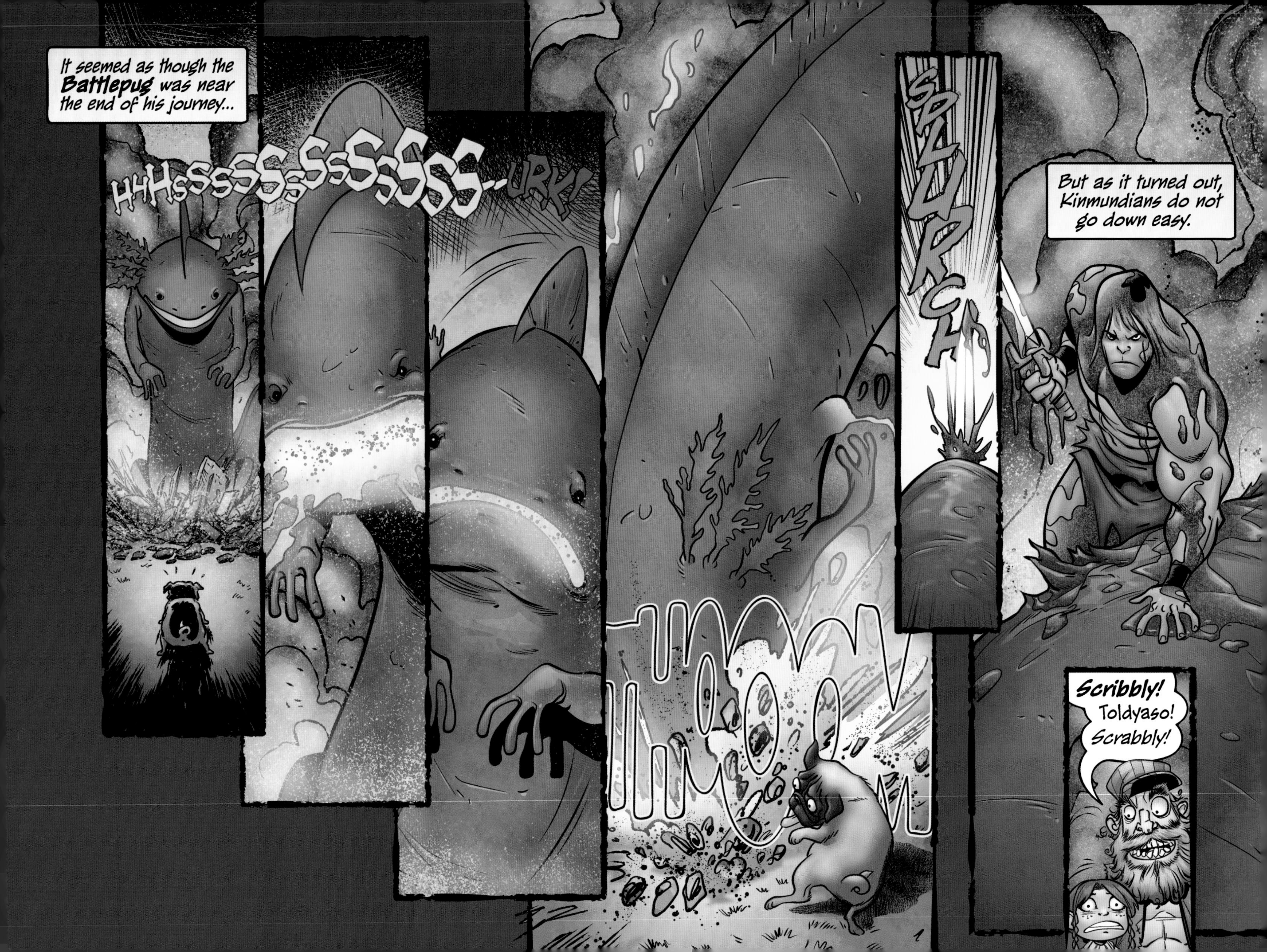

It seemed as though the **Battlepug** was near the end of his journey...
HHHsSSSSSsSSsSSsSSSS--URK!
SPLURCH
But as it turned out, Kinmundians do not go down easy.
Scribbly! Toldyaso! Scrabbly!

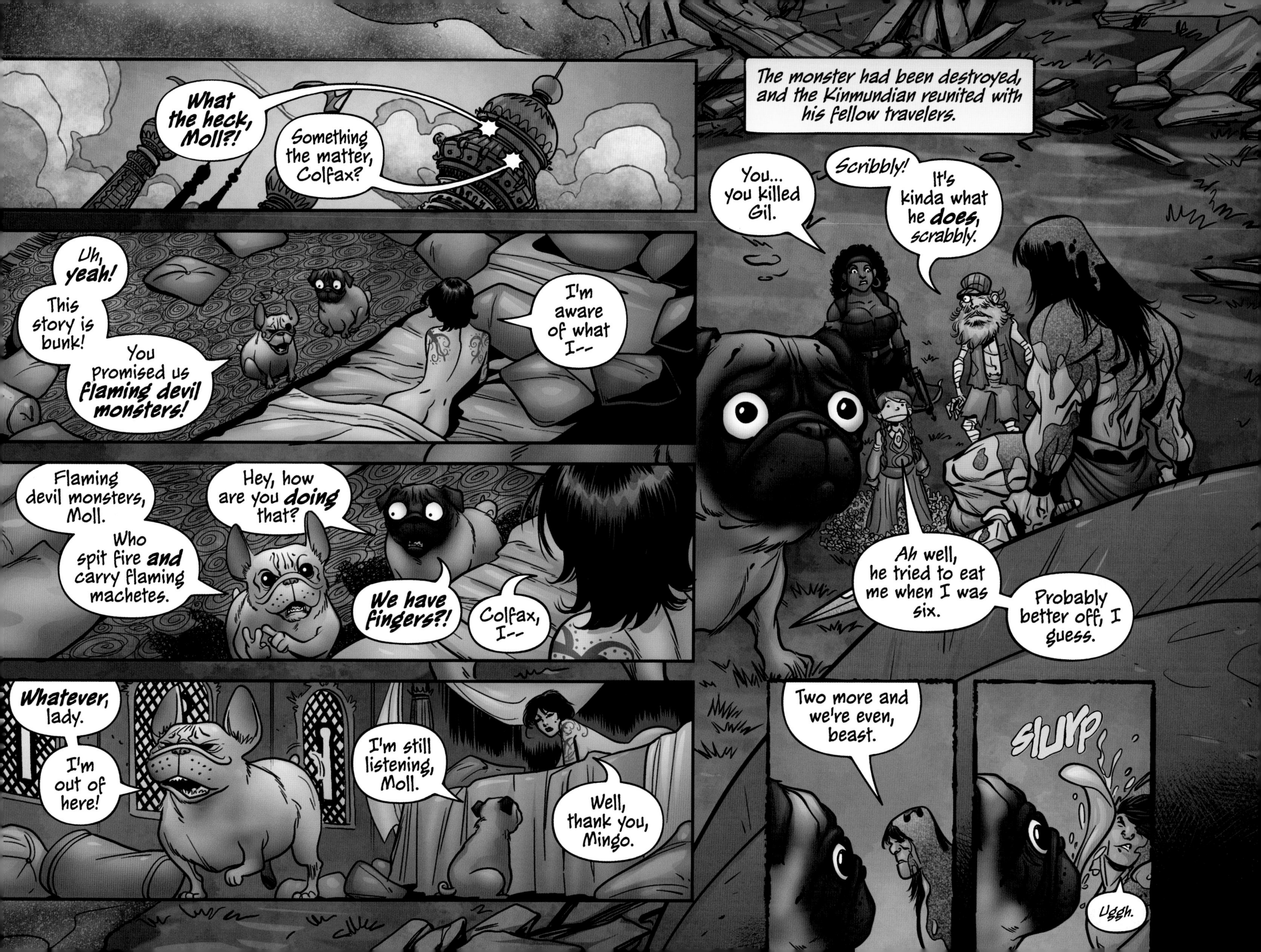
What the heck, Moll?!
Something the matter, Colfax?
Uh, yeah!
This story is bunk!
You promised us flaming devil monsters!
I'm aware of what I--
Flaming devil monsters, Moll.
Who spit fire and carry flaming machetes.
Hey, how are you doing that?
We have fingers?!
Colfax, I--
Whatever, lady.
I'm out of here!
I'm still listening, Moll.
Well, thank you, Mingo.
The monster had been destroyed, and the Kinmundian reunited with his fellow travelers.
You... you killed Gil.
Scribbly!
It's kinda what he does, scrabbly.
Ah well, he tried to eat me when I was six.
Probably better off, I guess.
Two more and we're even, beast.
SLURP
Uggh.

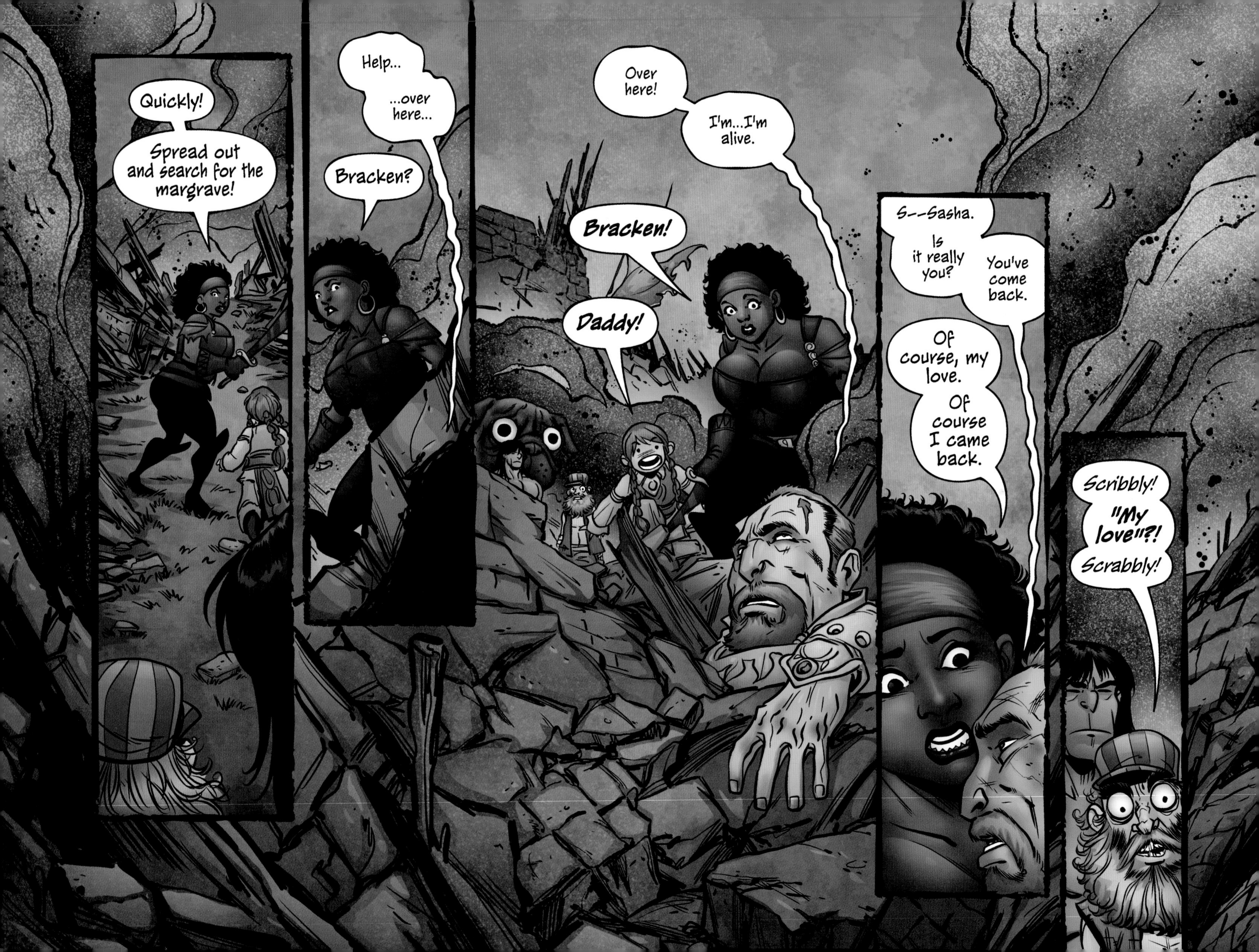
Quickly!
Spread out and search for the margrave!
Help...
...over here...
Bracken?
Over here!
I'm...I'm alive.
Bracken!
Daddy!
S--Sasha.
Is it really you?
You've come back.
Of course, my love.
Of course I came back.
Scribbly!
"My love"?!
Scrabbly!

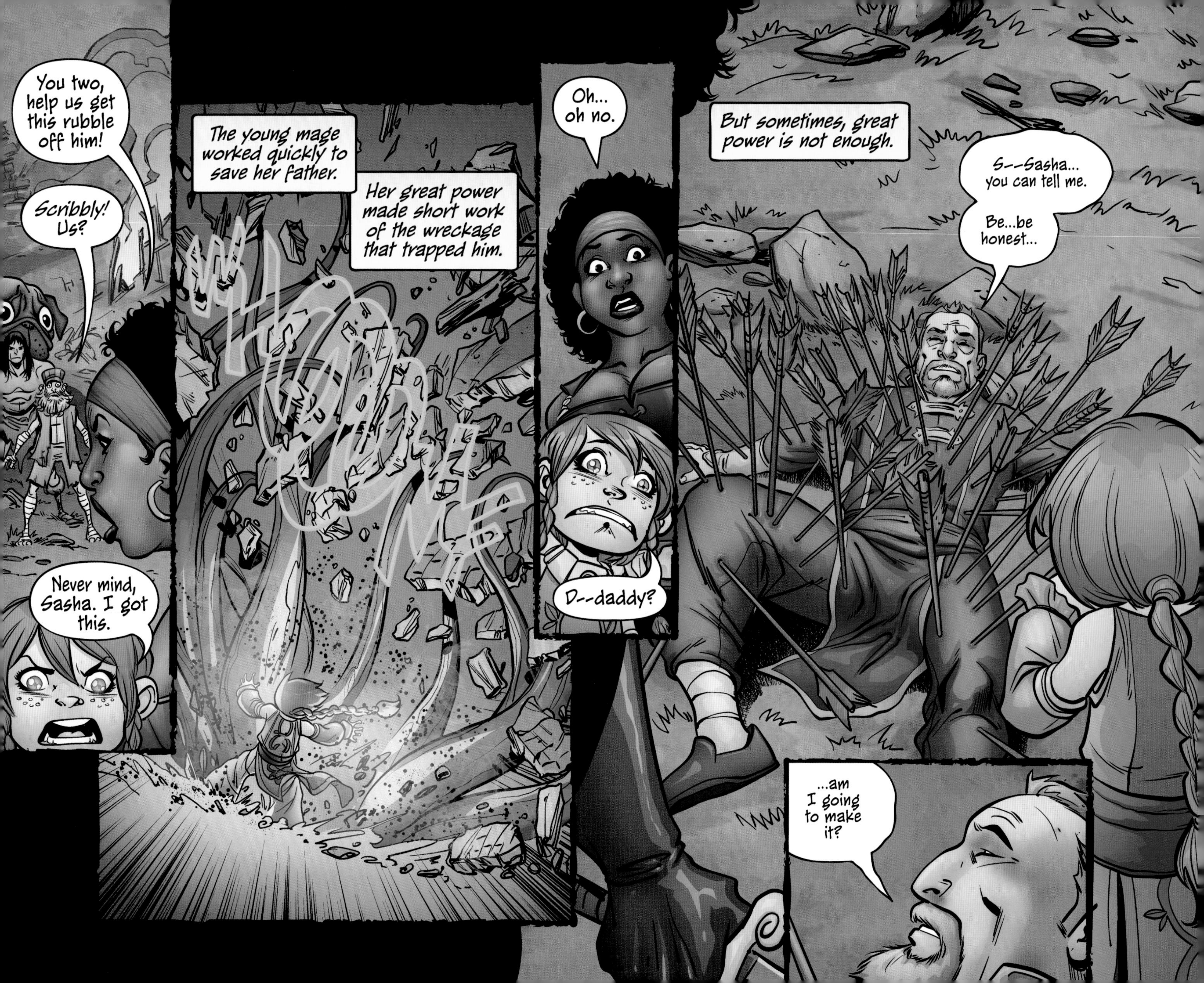
You two, help us get this rubble off him!
Scribbly! Us?
Never mind, Sasha. I got this.
The young mage worked quickly to save her father.
Her great power made short work of the wreckage that trapped him.
Oh... oh no.
D--daddy?
But sometimes, great power is not enough.
S--Sasha... you can tell me.
Be...be honest...
...am I going to make it?

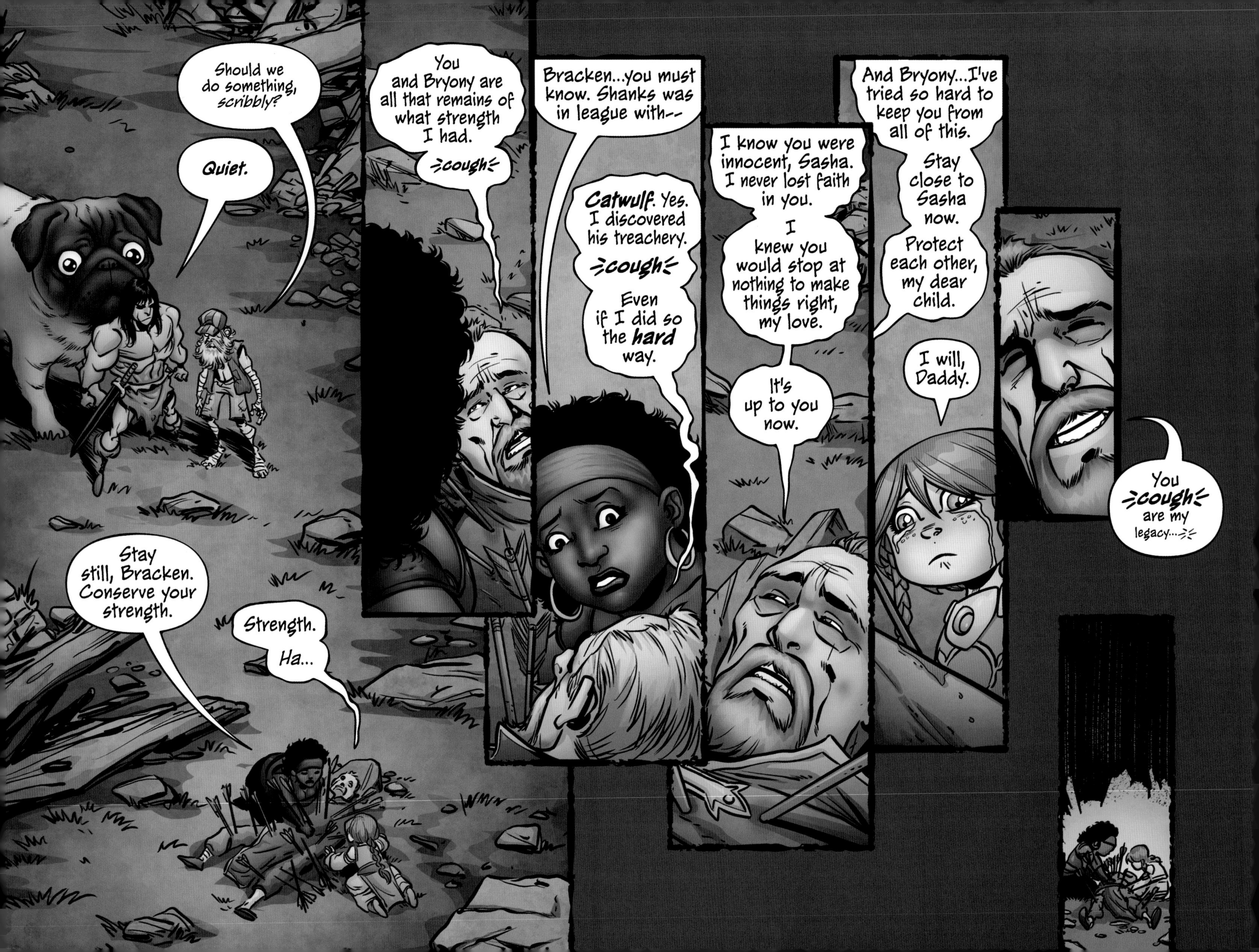
Should we do something, scribbly?
Quiet.
Stay still, Bracken. Conserve your strength.
Strength.
Ha...
You and Bryony are all that remains of what strength I had.
cough
Bracken...you must know. Shanks was in league with--
Catwulf. Yes. I discovered his treachery.
cough
Even if I did so the hard way.
I know you were innocent, Sasha. I never lost faith in you.
I knew you would stop at nothing to make things right, my love.
It's up to you now.
And Bryony...I've tried so hard to keep you from all of this.
Stay close to Sasha now.
Protect each other, my dear child.
I will, Daddy.
You cough are my legacy...

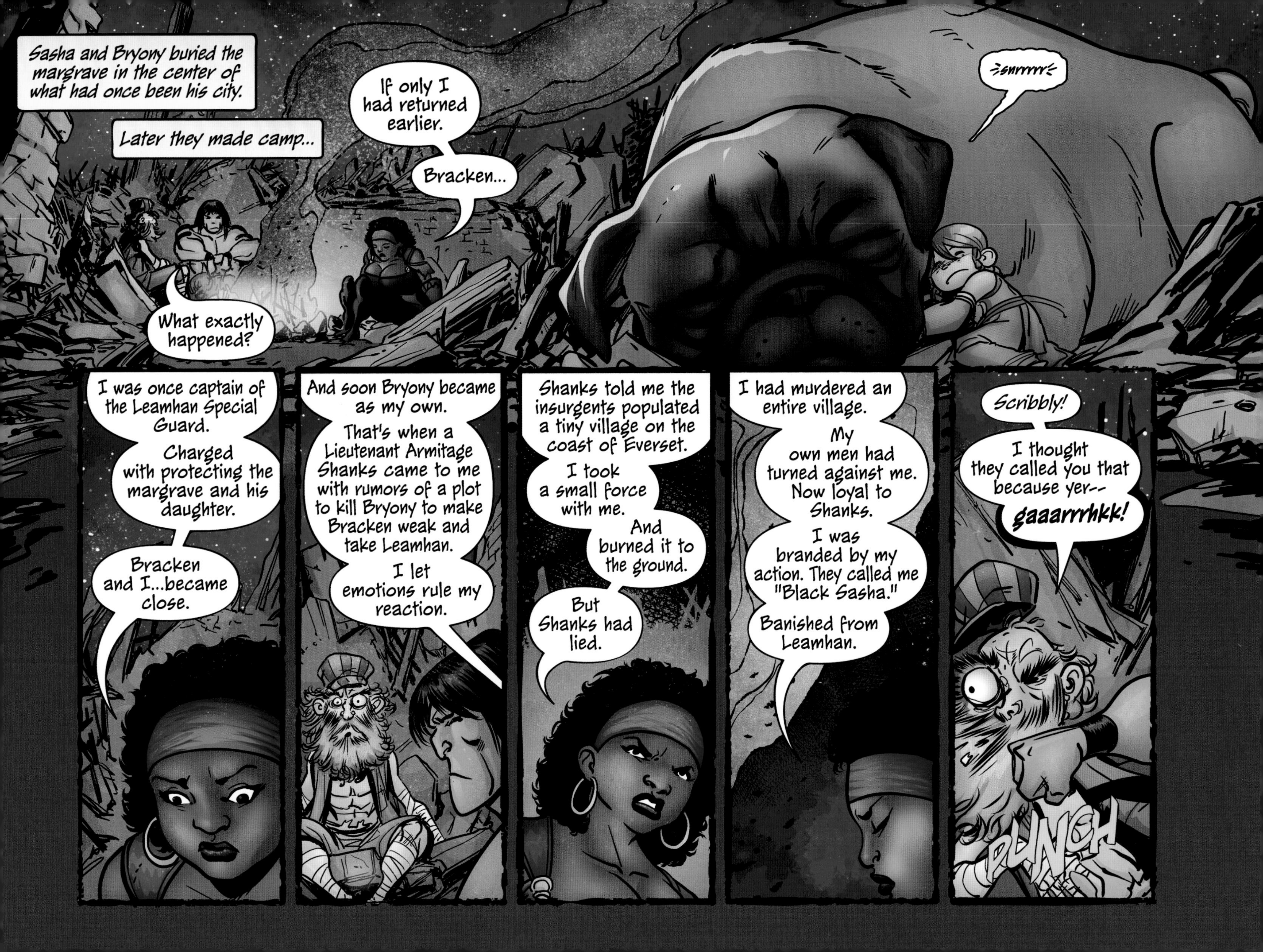

Sasha and Bryony buried the margrave in the center of what had once been his city.
Later they made camp...
If only I had returned earlier.
Bracken...
What exactly happened?
=snrrrrr=
I was once captain of the Leamhan Special Guard.
Charged with protecting the margrave and his daughter.
Bracken and I...became close.
And soon Bryony became as my own.
That's when a Lieutenant Armitage Shanks came to me with rumors of a plot to kill Bryony to make Bracken weak and take Leamhan.
I let emotions rule my reaction.
Shanks told me the insurgents populated a tiny village on the coast of Everset.
I took a small force with me.
And burned it to the ground.
But Shanks had lied.
I had murdered an entire village.
My own men had turned against me. Now loyal to Shanks.
I was branded by my action. They called me "Black Sasha."
Banished from Leamhan.
Scribbly!
I thought they called you that because yer--
gaaarrrhkk!
PUNCH

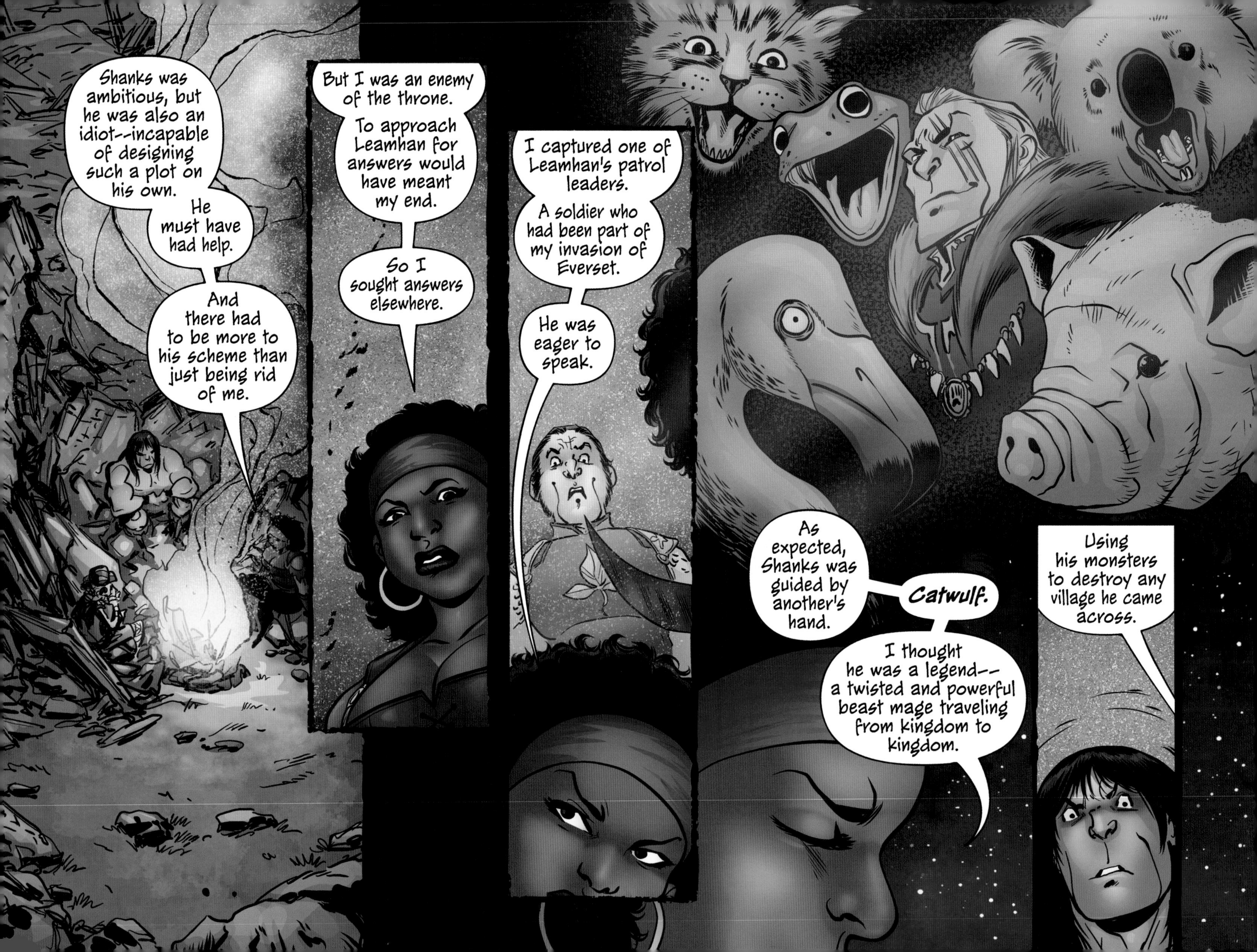
Shanks was ambitious, but he was also an idiot--incapable of designing such a plot on his own.
He must have had help.
And there had to be more to his scheme than just being rid of me.
But I was an enemy of the throne.
To approach Leamhan for answers would have meant my end.
So I sought answers elsewhere.
I captured one of Leamhan's patrol leaders.
A soldier who had been part of my invasion of Everset.
He was eager to speak.
As expected, Shanks was guided by another's hand.
Catwulf.
I thought he was a legend--a twisted and powerful beast mage traveling from kingdom to kingdom.
Using his monsters to destroy any village he came across.

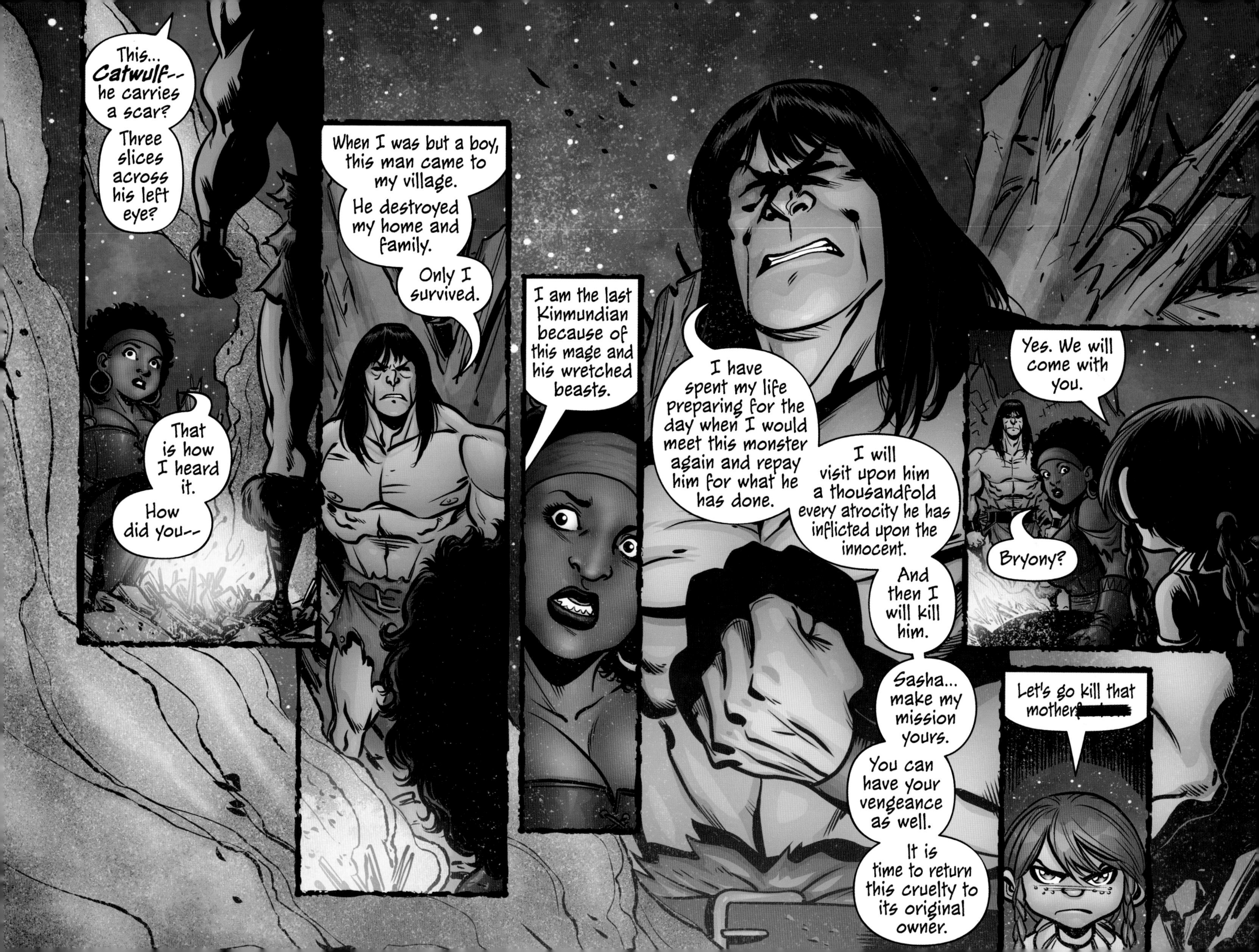

This... *Catwulf*-- he carries a scar?
Three slices across his left eye?
That is how I heard it.
How did you--
When I was but a boy, this man came to my village.
He destroyed my home and family.
Only I survived.
I am the last Kinmundian because of this mage and his wretched beasts.
I have spent my life preparing for the day when I would meet this monster again and repay him for what he has done.
I will visit upon him a thousandfold every atrocity he has inflicted upon the innocent.
And then I will kill him.
Sasha... make my mission yours.
You can have your vengeance as well.
It is time to return this cruelty to its original owner.
Yes. We will come with you.
Bryony?
Let's go kill that mother[redacted]

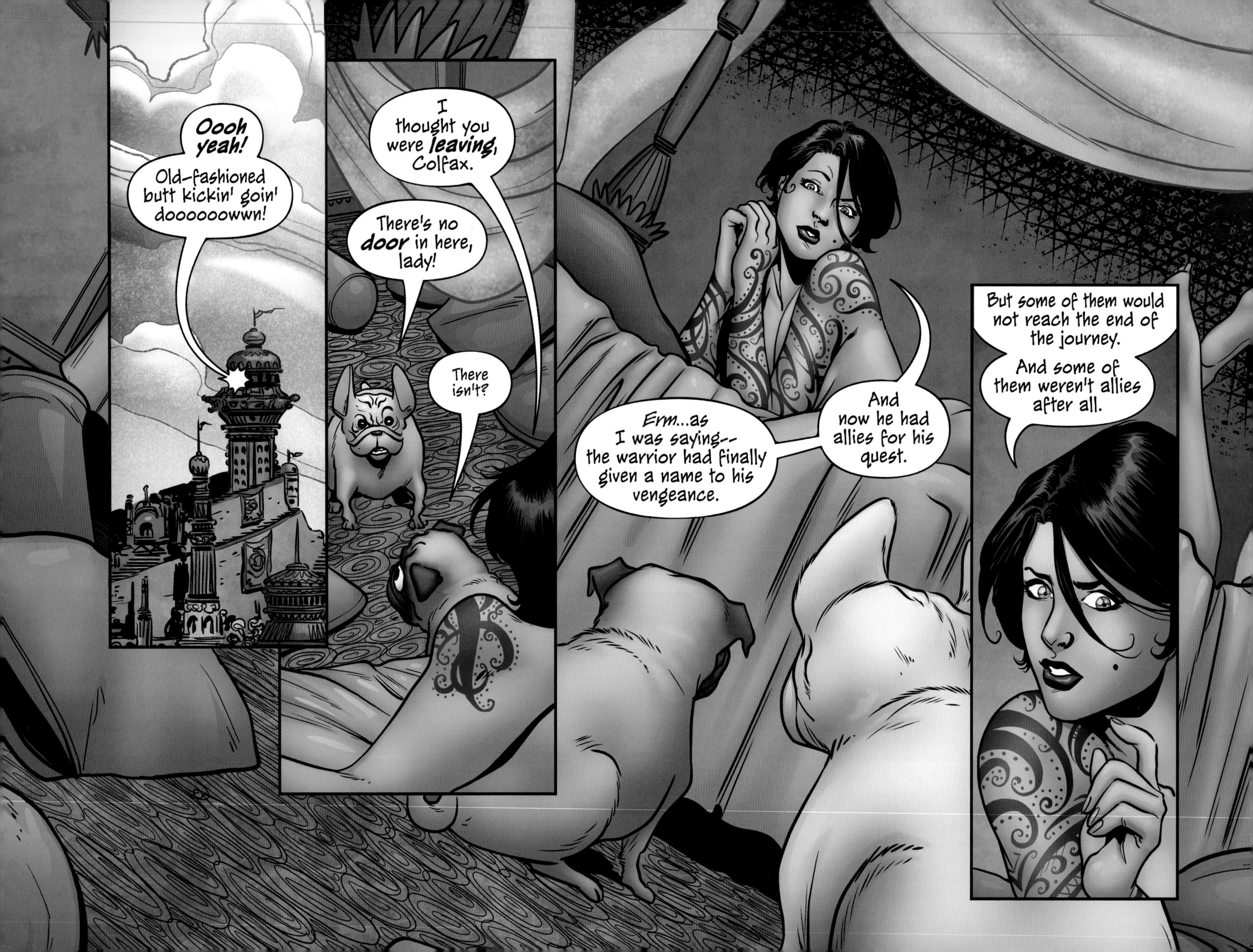
Oooh yeah! Old-fashioned butt kickin' goin' doooooowwn!
I thought you were leaving, Colfax.
There's no door in here, lady!
There isn't?
Erm...as I was saying-- the warrior had finally given a name to his vengeance.
And now he had allies for his quest.
But some of them would not reach the end of the journey.
And some of them weren't allies after all.

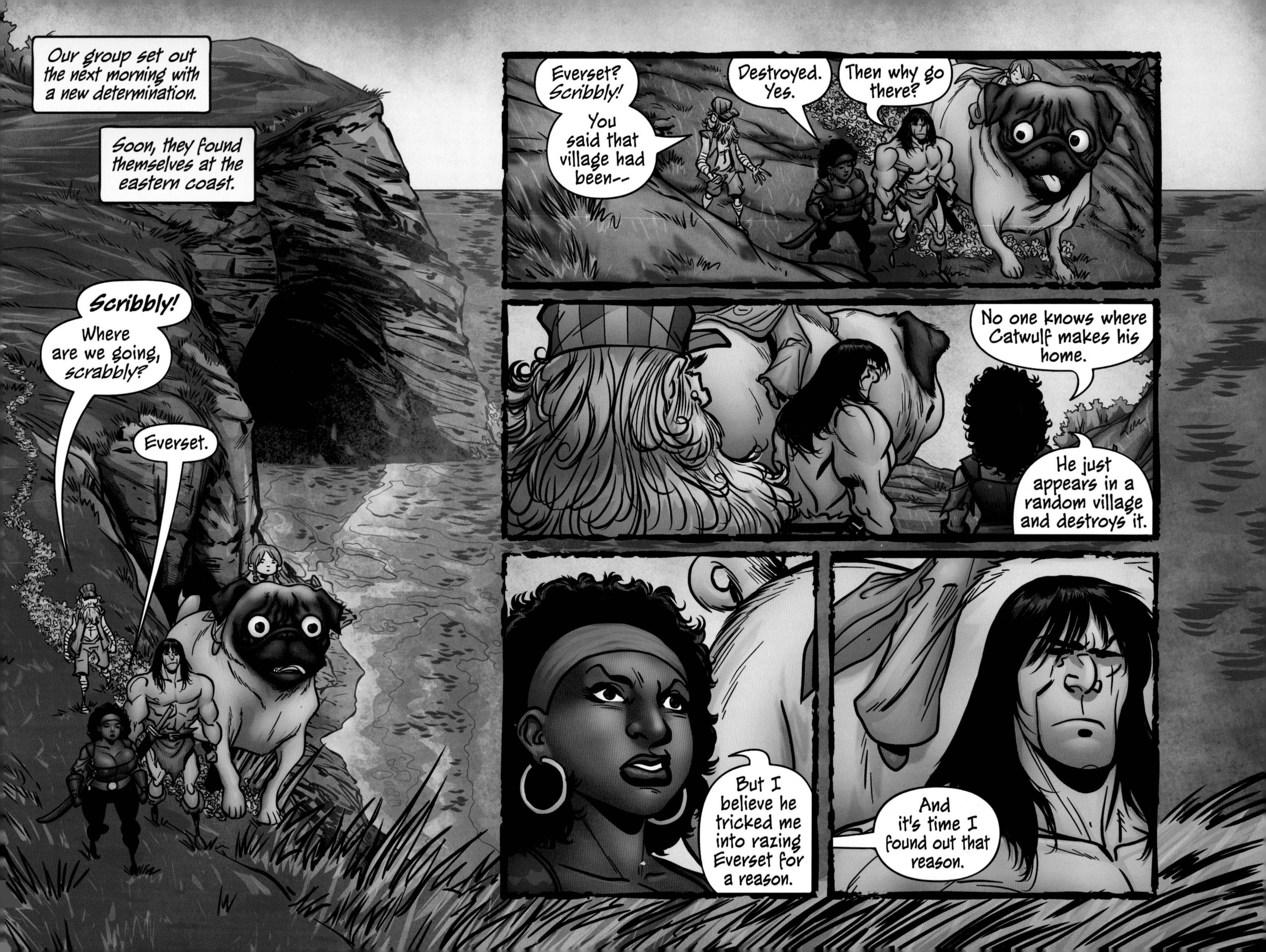
Our group set out the next morning with a new determination.
Soon, they found themselves at the eastern coast.
Scribbly!
Where are we going, scrabbly?
Everset.
Everset? Scribbly!
You said that village had been--
Destroyed. Yes.
Then why go there?
No one knows where Catwulf makes his home.
He just appears in a random village and destroys it.
But I believe he tricked me into razing Everset for a reason.
And it's time I found out that reason.

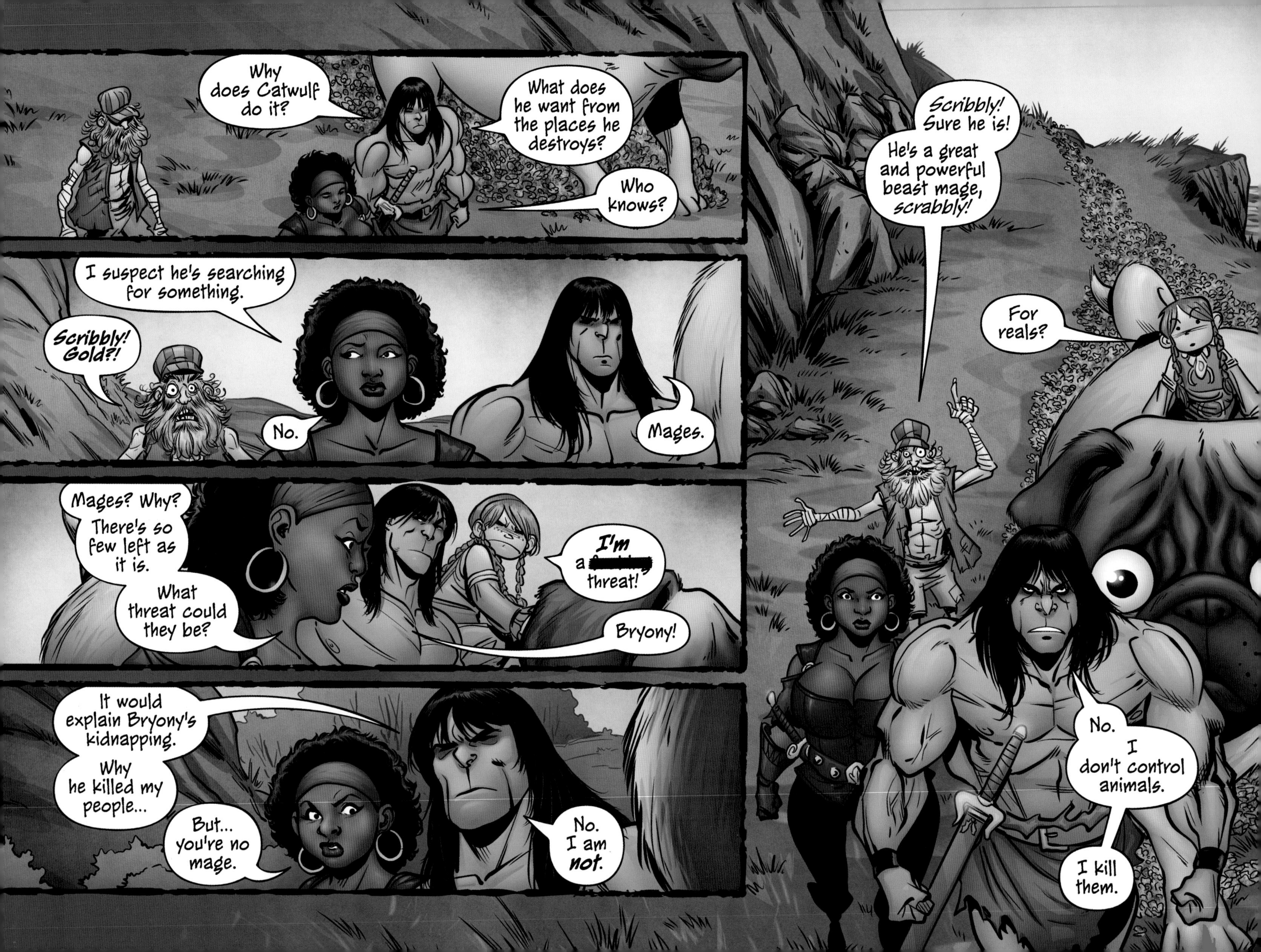

Why does Catwulf do it?
What does he want from the places he destroys?
Who knows?
I suspect he's searching for something.
Scribbly! Gold?!
No.
Mages.
Mages? Why?
There's so few left as it is.
What threat could they be?
I'm a [redacted] threat!
Bryony!
It would explain Bryony's kidnapping.
Why he killed my people...
But... you're no mage.
No. I am not.
Scribbly! Sure he is!
He's a great and powerful beast mage, scrabbly!
For reals?
No.
I don't control animals.
I kill them.

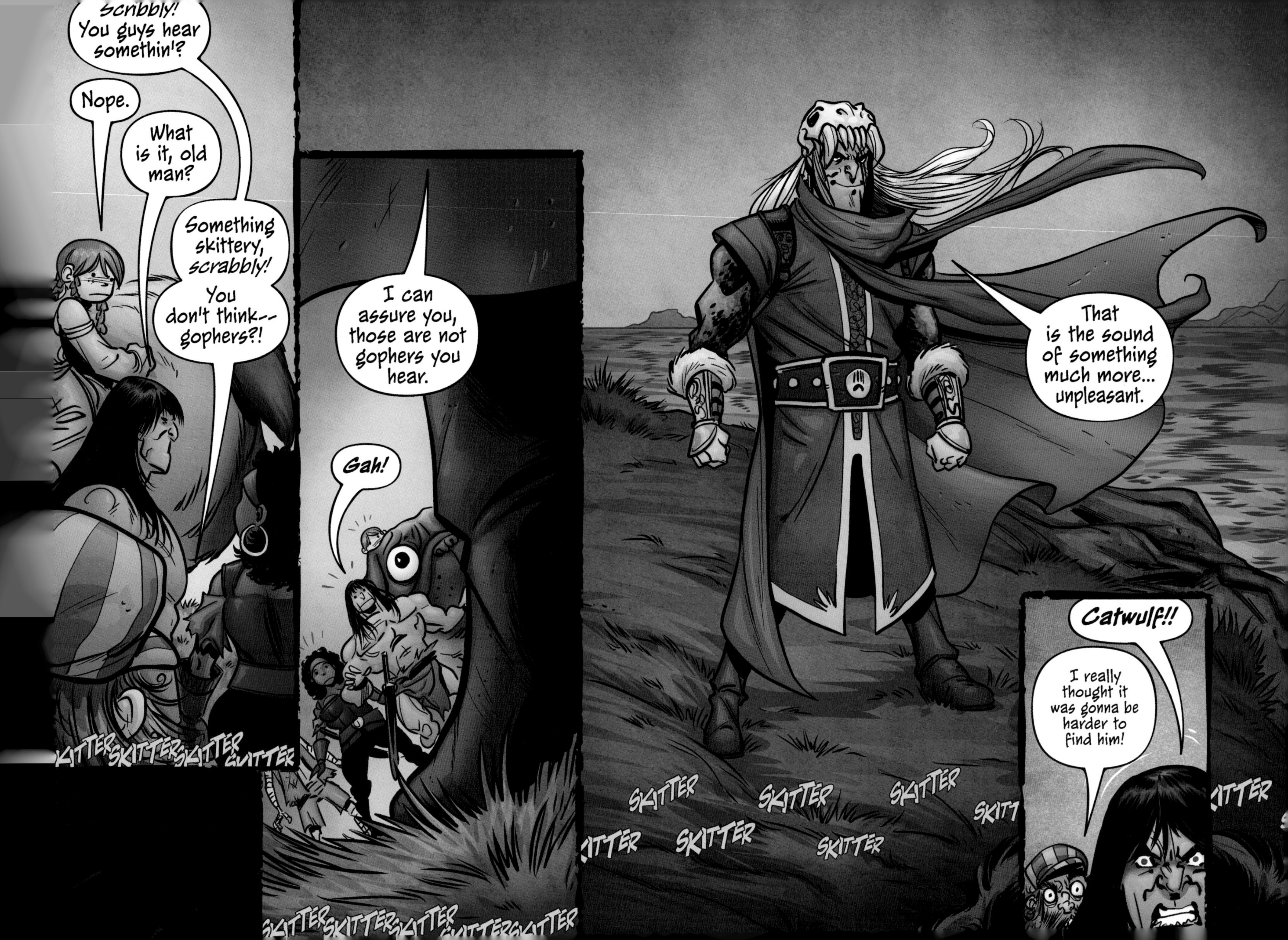
Scribbly! You guys hear somethin'?
Nope.
What is it, old man?
Something skittery, scrabbly!
You don't think--gophers?!
SKITTER SKITTER SKITTER SKITTER
I can assure you, those are not gophers you hear.
Gah!
SKITTER SKITTER SKITTER SKITTER SKITTER
That is the sound of something much more... unpleasant.
SKITTER SKITTER SKITTER SKITTER SKITTER SKITTER
Catwulf!!
I really thought it was gonna be harder to find him!

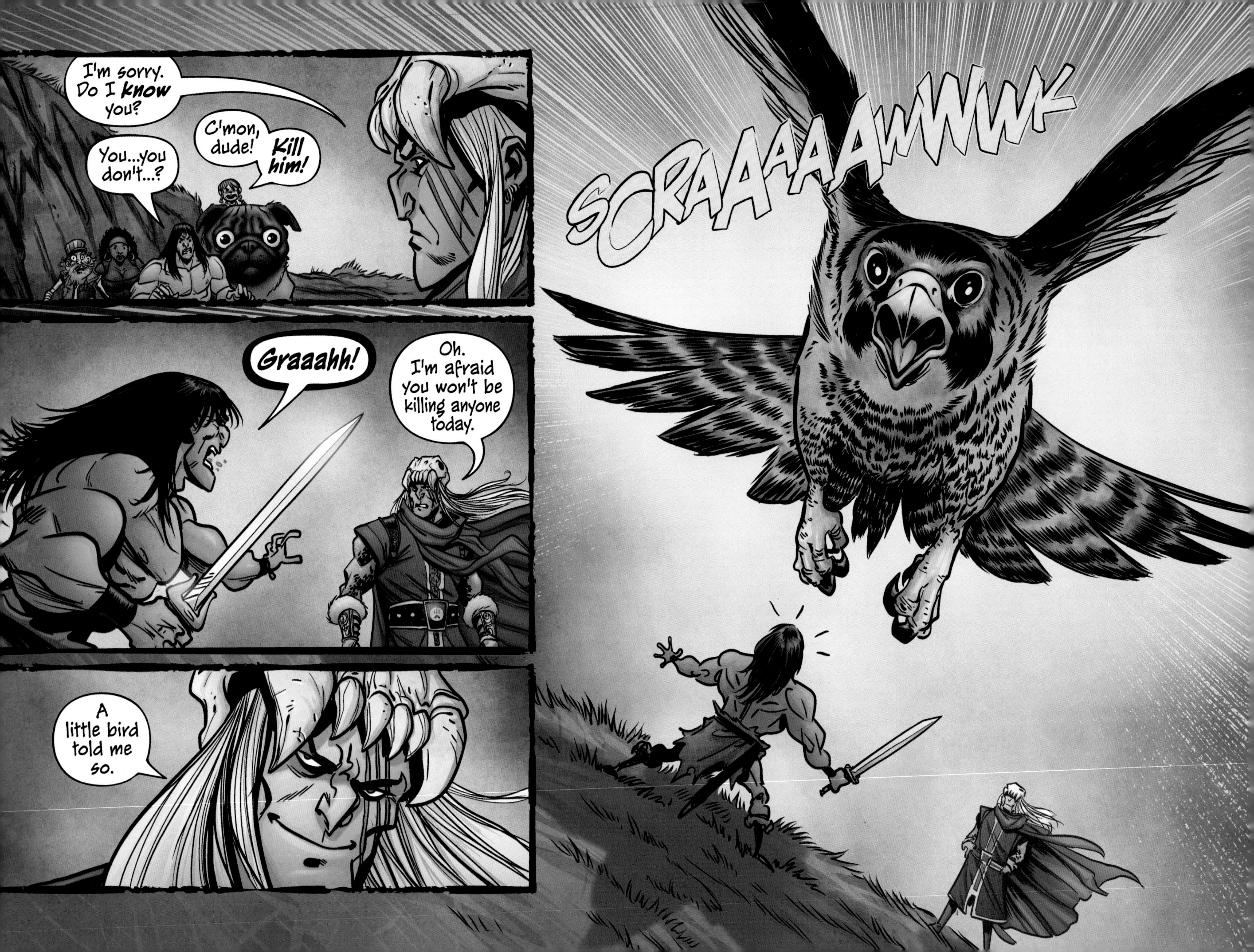

I'm sorry. Do I **know** you?
You...you don't...?
C'mon, dude! **Kill him!**
Graaahh!
Oh. I'm afraid you won't be killing anyone today.
A little bird told me so.
SCRAAAAAWWWK

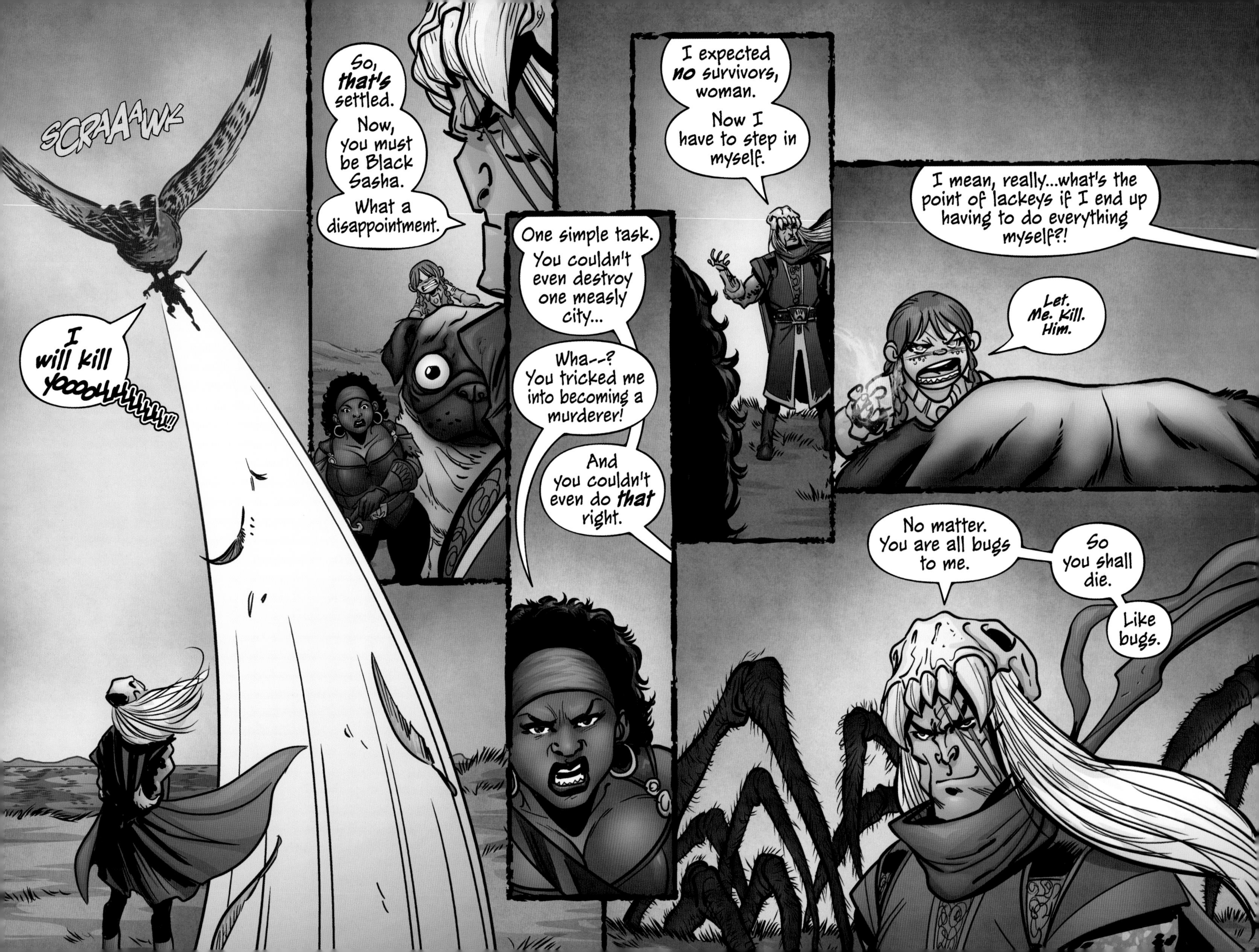
SCRAAAWK
I will kill yoooouuuuuu!!
So, that's settled.
Now, you must be Black Sasha.
What a disappointment.
One simple task.
You couldn't even destroy one measly city...
Wha--? You tricked me into becoming a murderer!
And you couldn't even do that right.
I expected no survivors, woman.
Now I have to step in myself.
I mean, really...what's the point of lackeys if I end up having to do everything myself?!
Let. Me. Kill. Him.
No matter. You are all bugs to me.
So you shall die.
Like bugs.

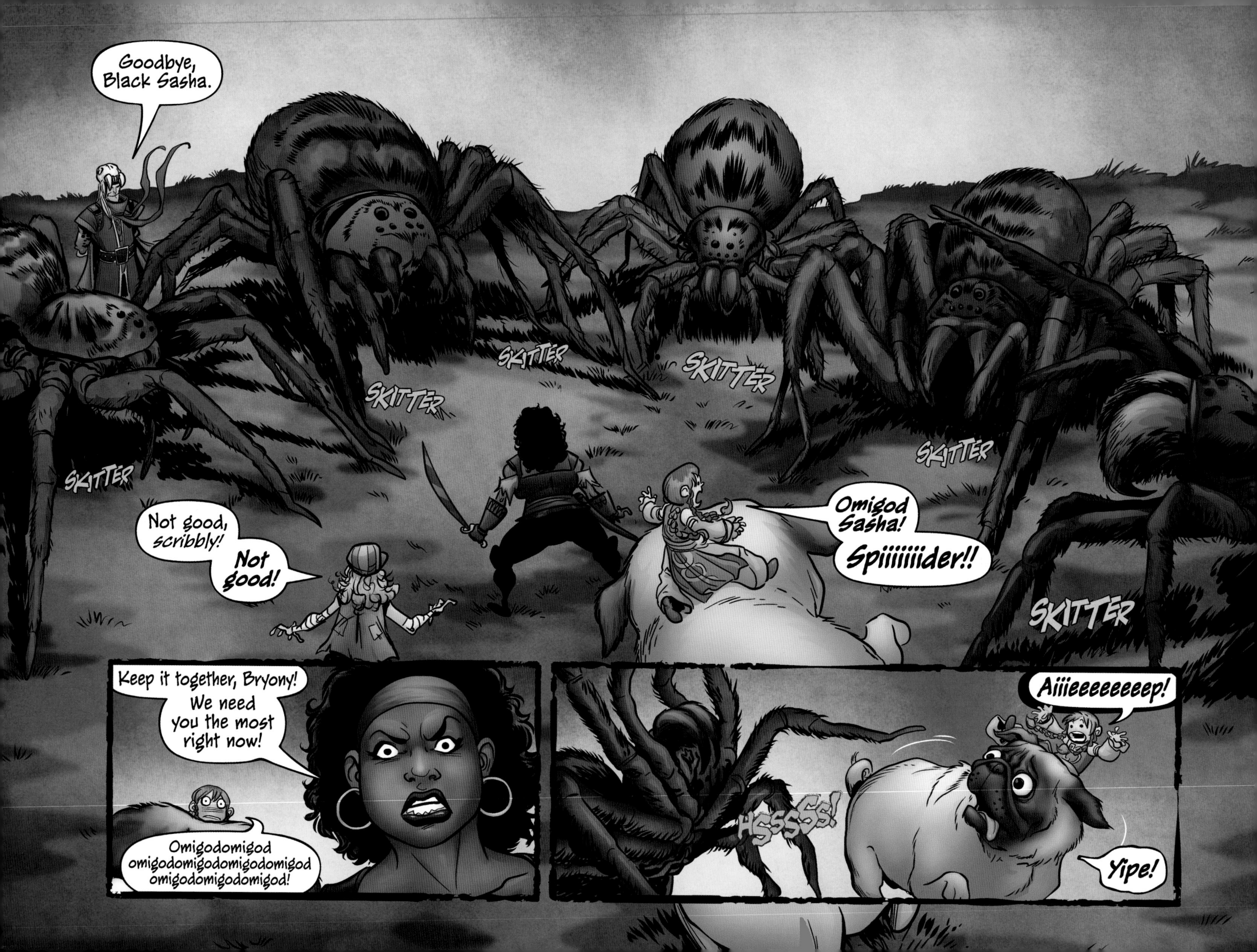

Goodbye, Black Sasha.
SKITTER
SKITTER
SKITTER
SKITTER
SKITTER
Not good, scribbly! Not good!
Omigod Sasha! Spiiiiiiider!!
SKITTER
Keep it together, Bryony! We need you the most right now!
Omigodomigod omigodomigodomigodomigod omigodomigodomigod!
Aiiieeeeeeeep!
HSSSSS!
Yipe!

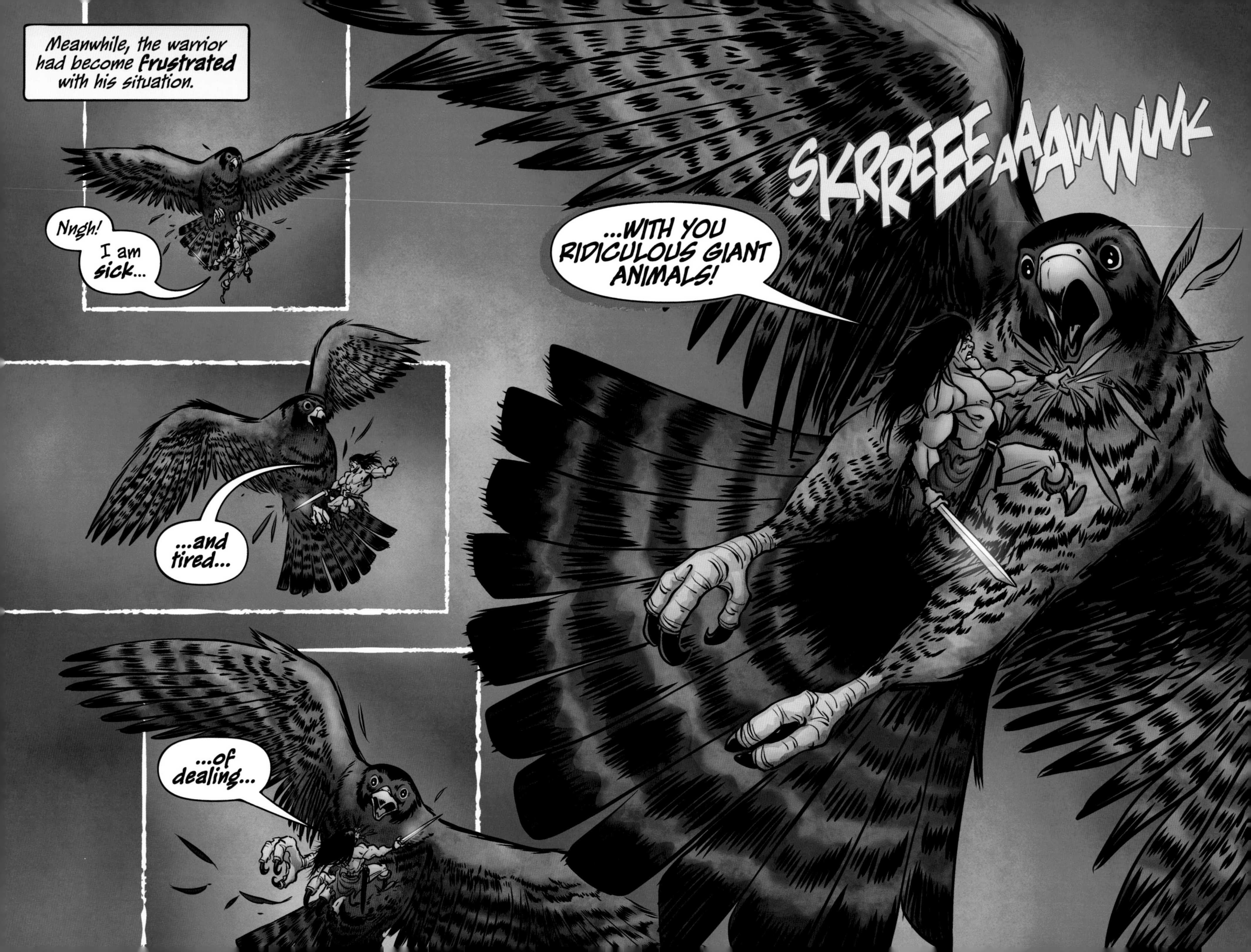
Meanwhile, the warrior had become **frustrated** with his situation.
Nngh! I am sick...
...and tired...
...of dealing...
SKREEEAAAWWWK
...WITH YOU RIDICULOUS GIANT ANIMALS!

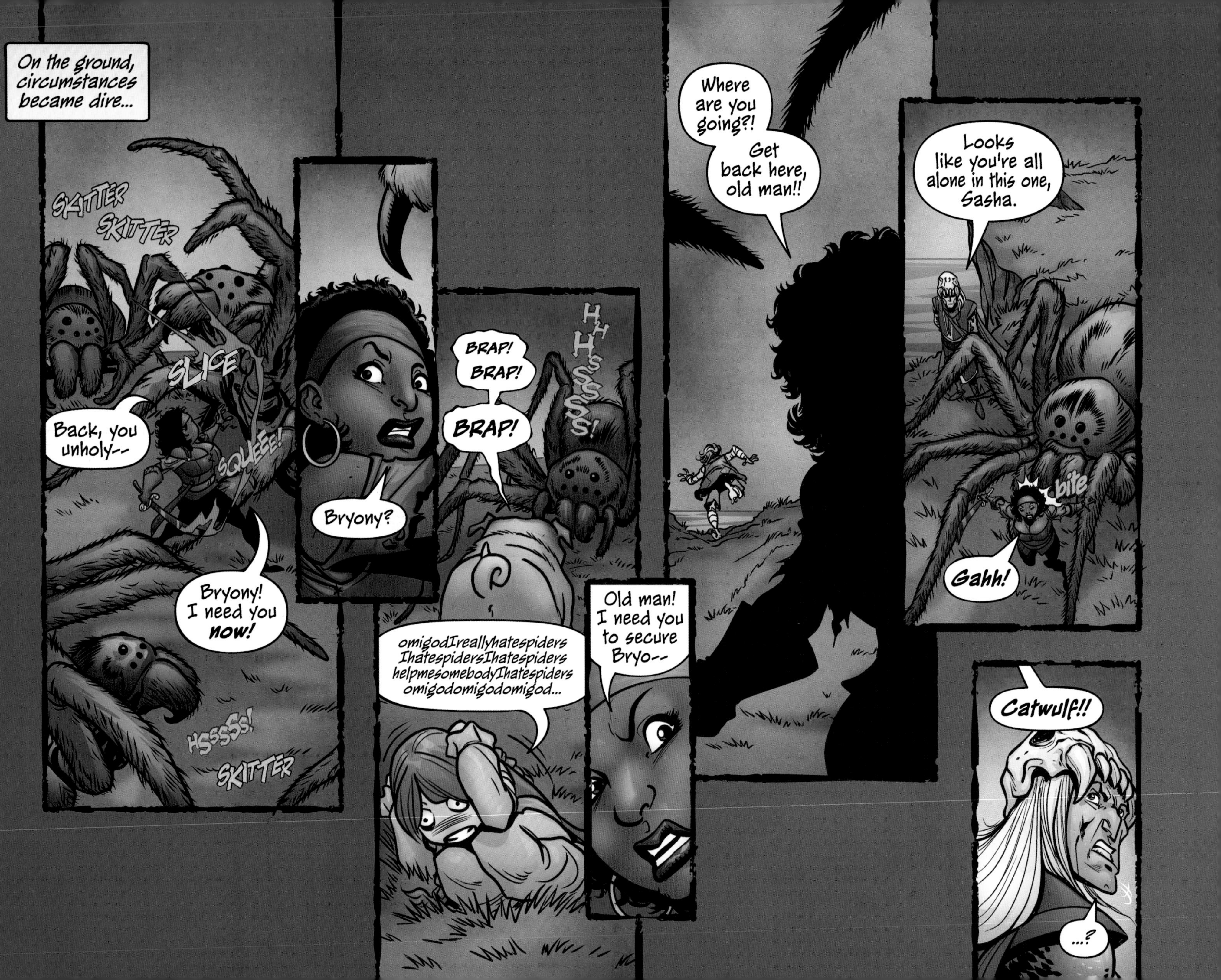

On the ground, circumstances became dire...
SKITTER SKITTER
SLICE
SQUEEE!
Back, you unholy--
Bryony! I need you now!
HSSSSS!
SKITTER
Bryony?
BRAP! BRAP! BRAP!
HHHSSSSS!
omigodIreallyhatespiders IhatespidersIhatespiders helpmesomebodyIhatespiders omigodomigodomigod...
Old man! I need you to secure Bryo--
Where are you going?!
Get back here, old man!!
Looks like you're all alone in this one, Sasha.
bite
Gahh!
Catwulf!!
...?

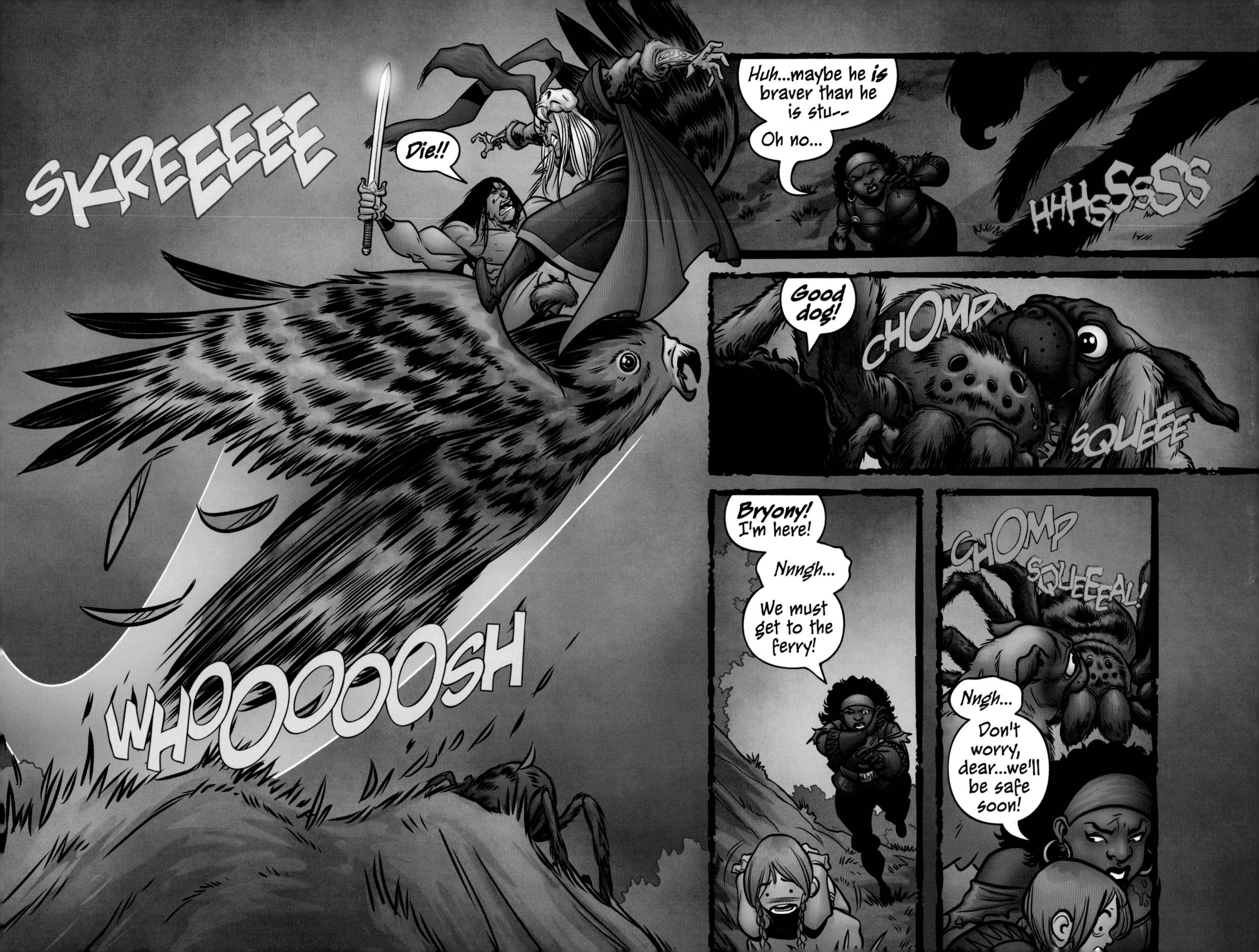
SKREEEEEE
Die!!
WHOOOOOOOSH
Huh...maybe he is braver than he is stu--
Oh no...
HHHSSSSS
Good dog!
CHOMP
SQUEEE
Bryony! I'm here!
Nnngh...
We must get to the ferry!
CHOMP
SQUEEEAL!
Nngh...
Don't worry, dear...we'll be safe soon!

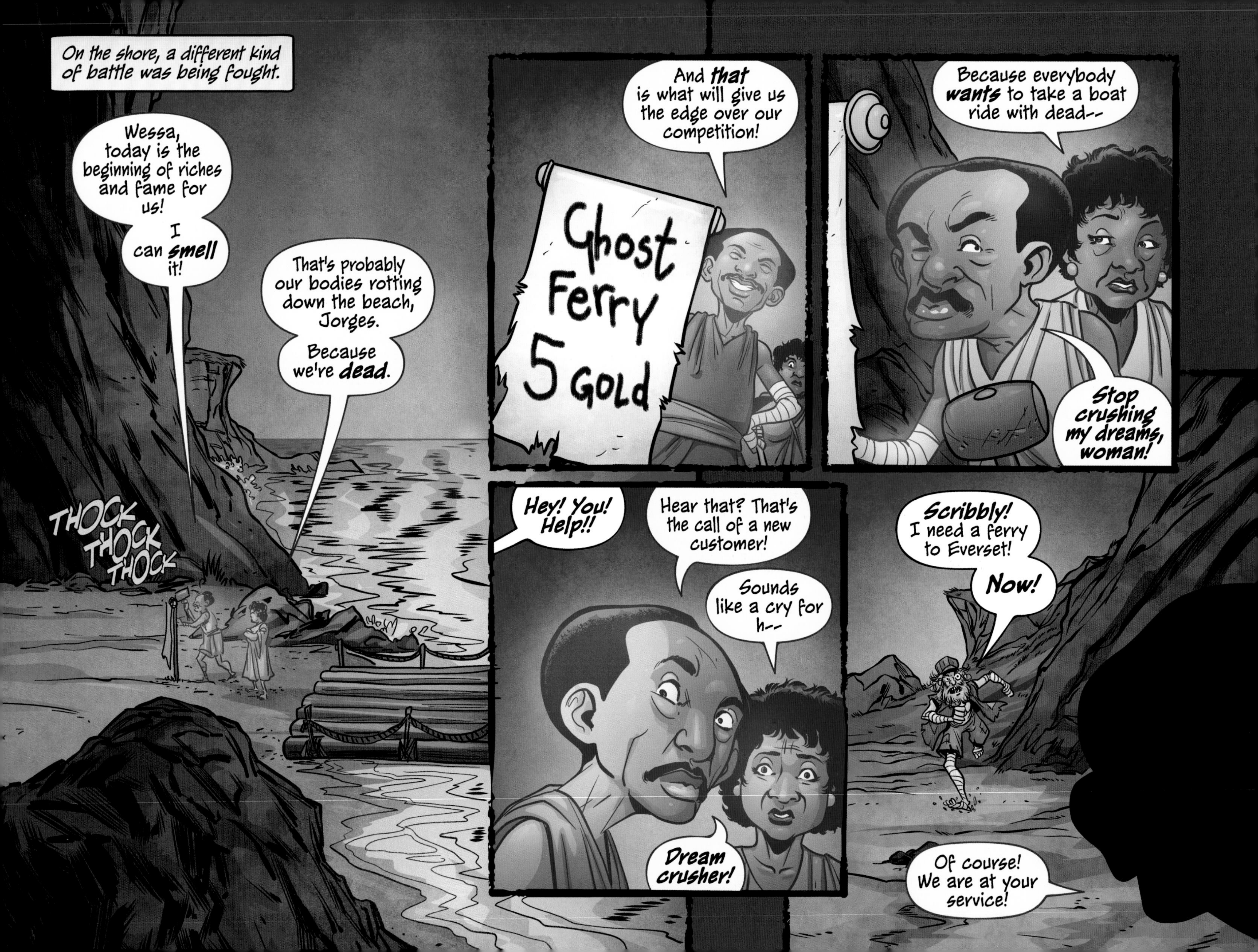

On the shore, a different kind of battle was being fought.
Wessa, today is the beginning of riches and fame for us!
I can smell it!
That's probably our bodies rotting down the beach, Jorges.
Because we're dead.
THOCK THOCK THOCK
And that is what will give us the edge over our competition!
Ghost Ferry 5 Gold
Because everybody wants to take a boat ride with dead--
Stop crushing my dreams, woman!
Hey! You! Help!!
Hear that? That's the call of a new customer!
Sounds like a cry for h--
Dream crusher!
Scribbly! I need a ferry to Everset!
Now!
Of course! We are at your service!

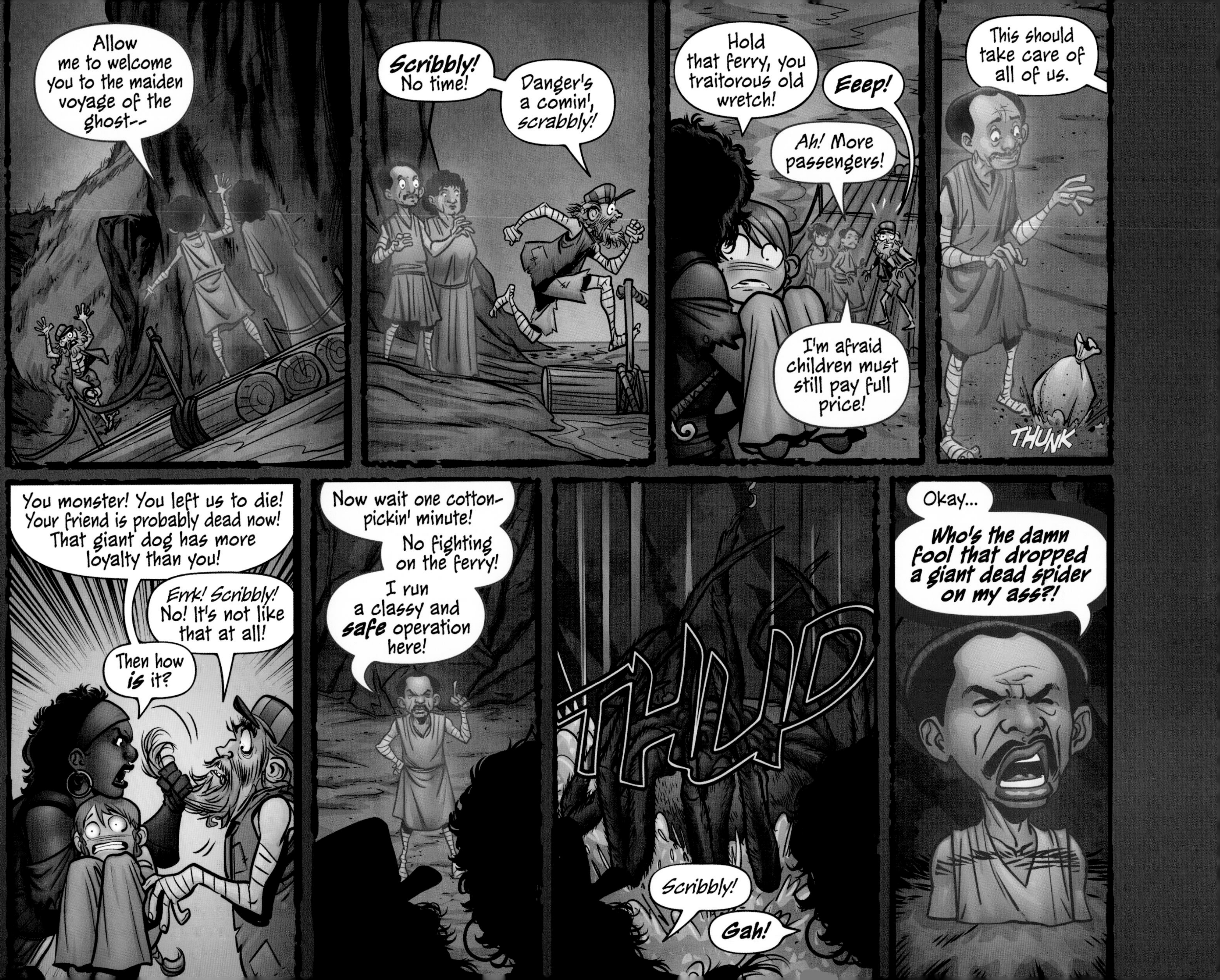

Allow me to welcome you to the maiden voyage of the ghost--
Scribbly! No time!
Danger's a comin', scrabbly!
Hold that ferry, you traitorous old wretch!
Eeep!
Ah! More passengers!
I'm afraid children must still pay full price!
This should take care of all of us.
THUNK
You monster! You left us to die! Your friend is probably dead now! That giant dog has more loyalty than you!
Errk! Scribbly! No! It's not like that at all!
Then how is it?
Now wait one cotton-pickin' minute!
No fighting on the ferry!
I run a classy and safe operation here!
THUD
Scribbly!
Gah!
Okay...
Who's the damn fool that dropped a giant dead spider on my ass?!

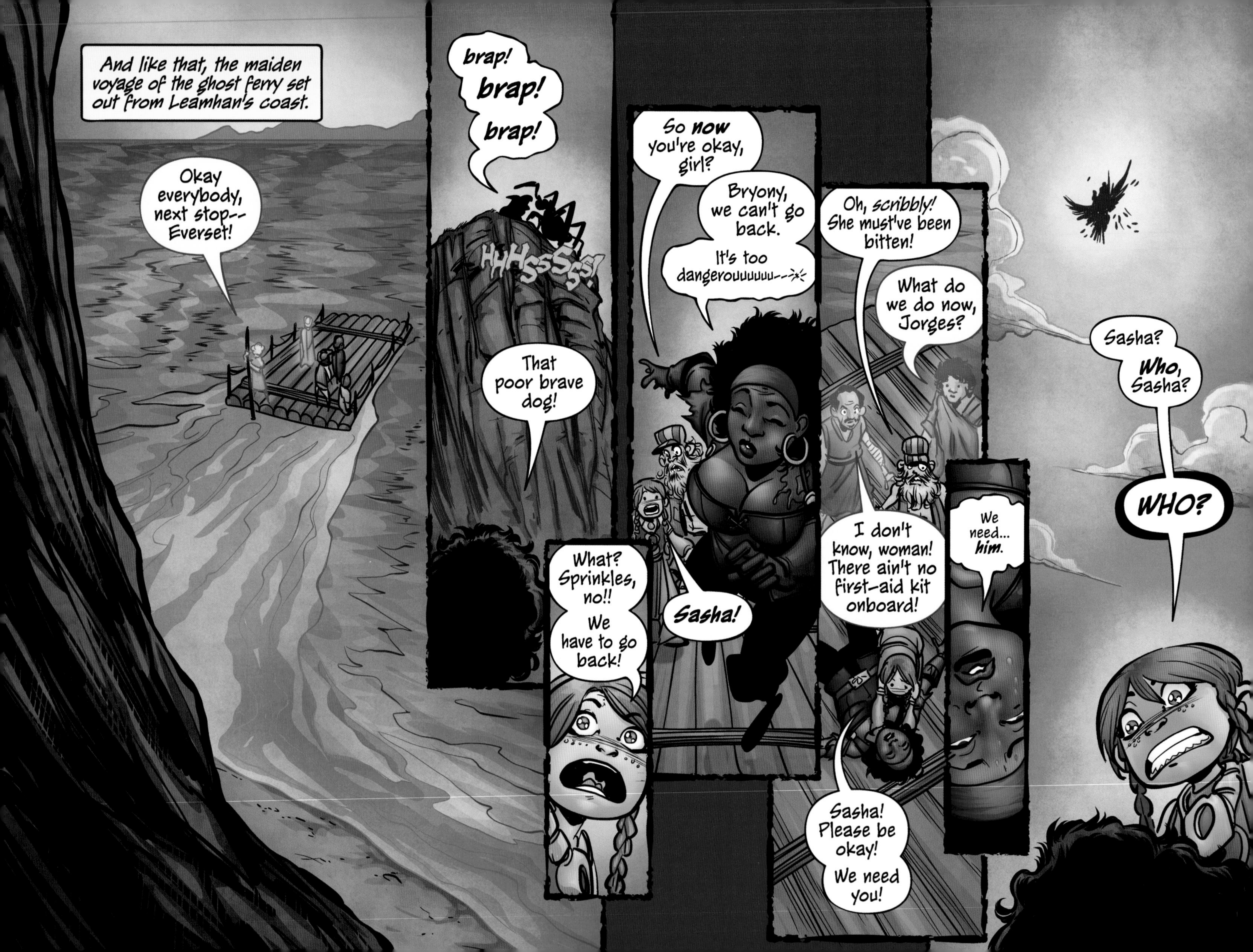

And like that, the maiden voyage of the ghost ferry set out from Leamhan's coast.
Okay everybody, next stop-- Everset!
brap! brap! brap!
HHHSSSSS!
That poor brave dog!
What? Sprinkles, no!! We have to go back!
So now you're okay, girl?
Bryony, we can't go back.
It's too dangerouuuuuu--
Sasha!
Oh, scribbly! She must've been bitten!
What do we do now, Jorges?
I don't know, woman! There ain't no first-aid kit onboard!
Sasha! Please be okay! We need you!
We need... him.
Sasha? Who, Sasha?
WHO?

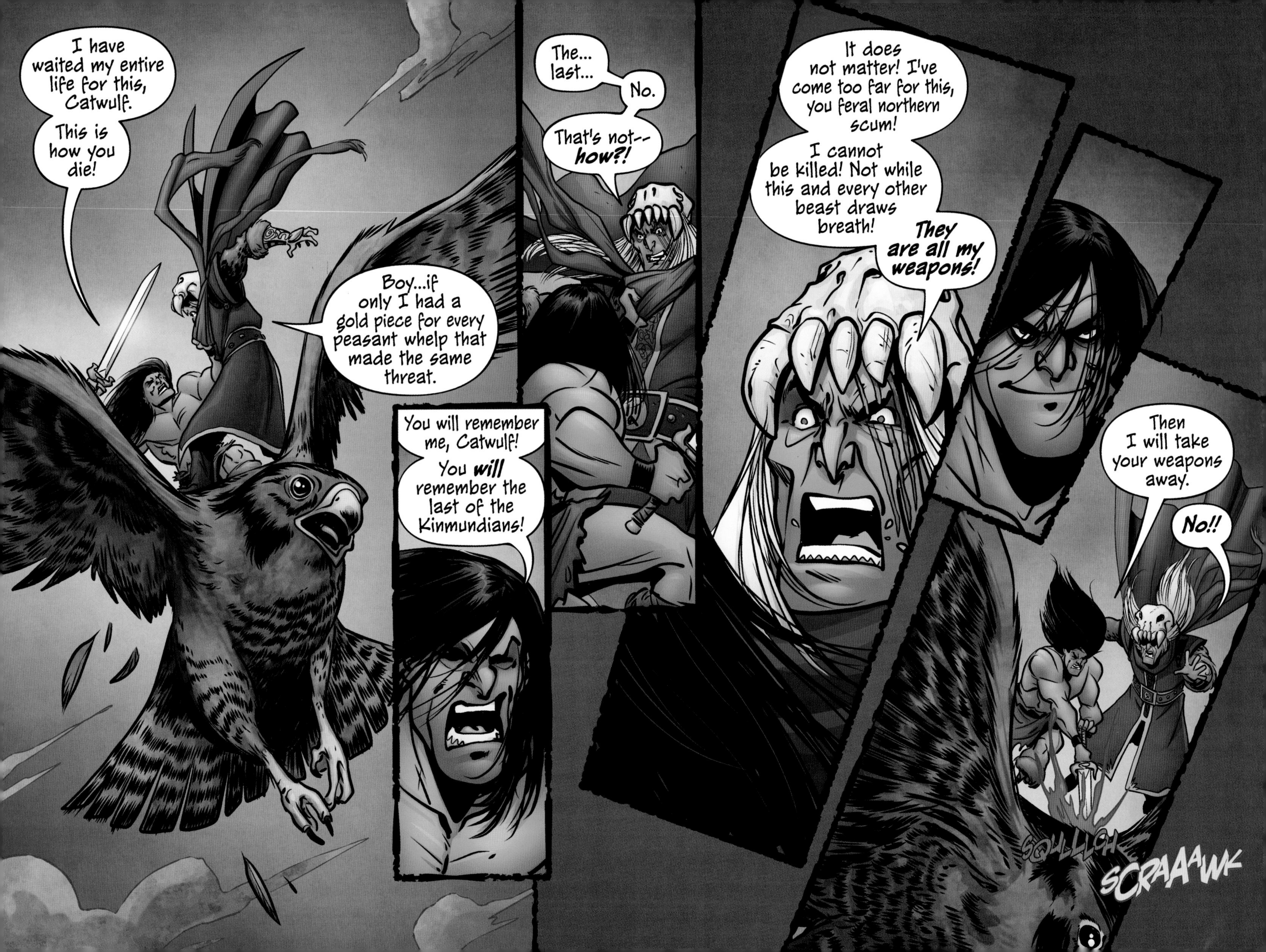
I have waited my entire life for this, Catwulf.
This is how you die!
Boy...if only I had a gold piece for every peasant whelp that made the same threat.
You will remember me, Catwulf!
You *will* remember the last of the Kinmundians!
The... last...
No.
That's not-- ***how?!***
It does not matter! I've come too far for this, you feral northern scum!
I cannot be killed! Not while this and every other beast draws breath!
They are all my weapons!
Then I will take your weapons away.
No!!
SQLLCH
SCRAAAWK

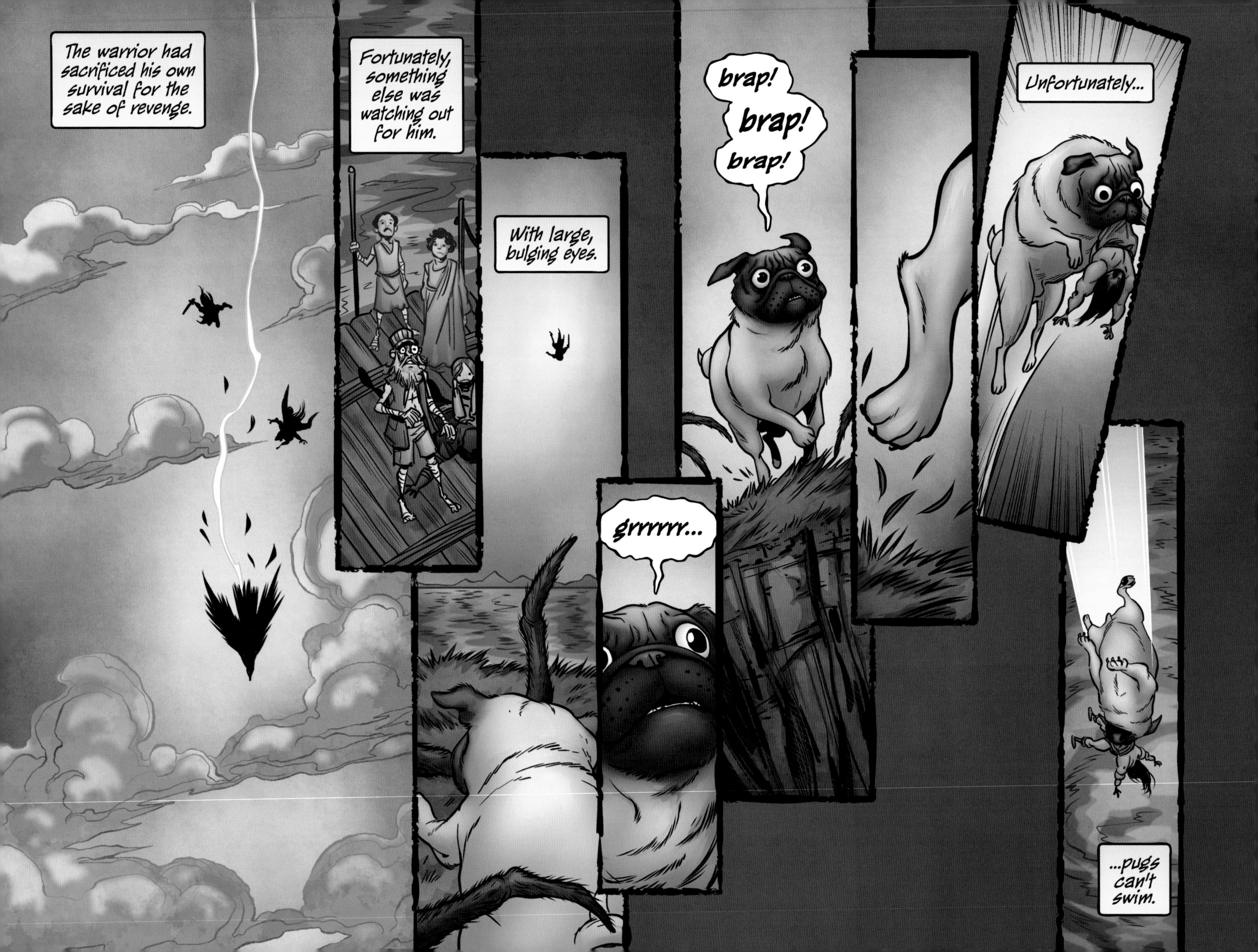
The warrior had sacrificed his own survival for the sake of revenge.
Fortunately, something else was watching out for him.
With large, bulging eyes.
grrrrrr...
brap!
brap!
brap!
Unfortunately...
...pugs can't swim.

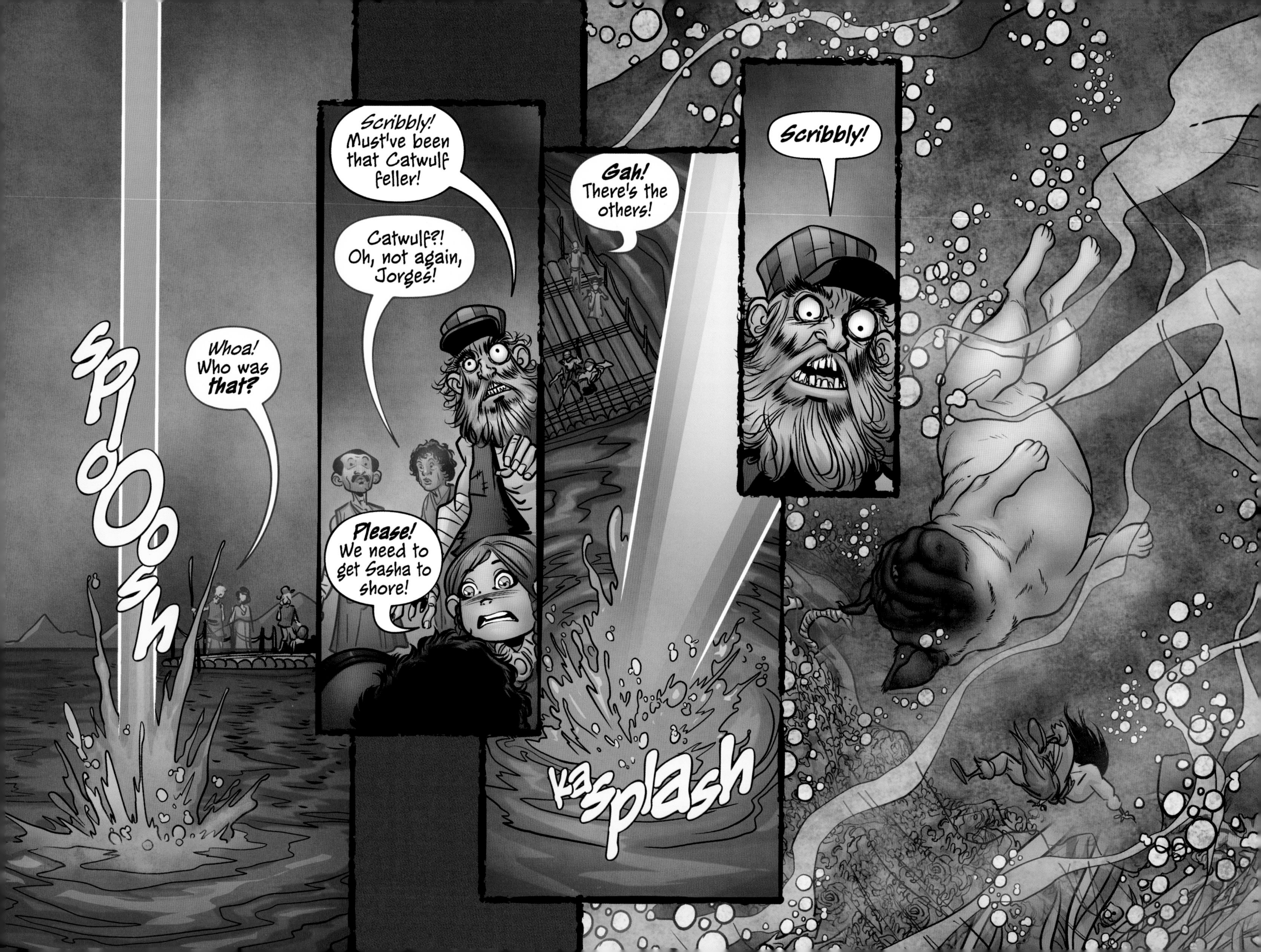
SPLOOOSH
Whoa! Who was *that?*
Scribbly! Must've been that Catwulf feller!
Catwulf?! Oh, not again, Jorges!
Please! We need to get Sasha to shore!
Gah! There's the others!
KASPLASH
Scribbly!

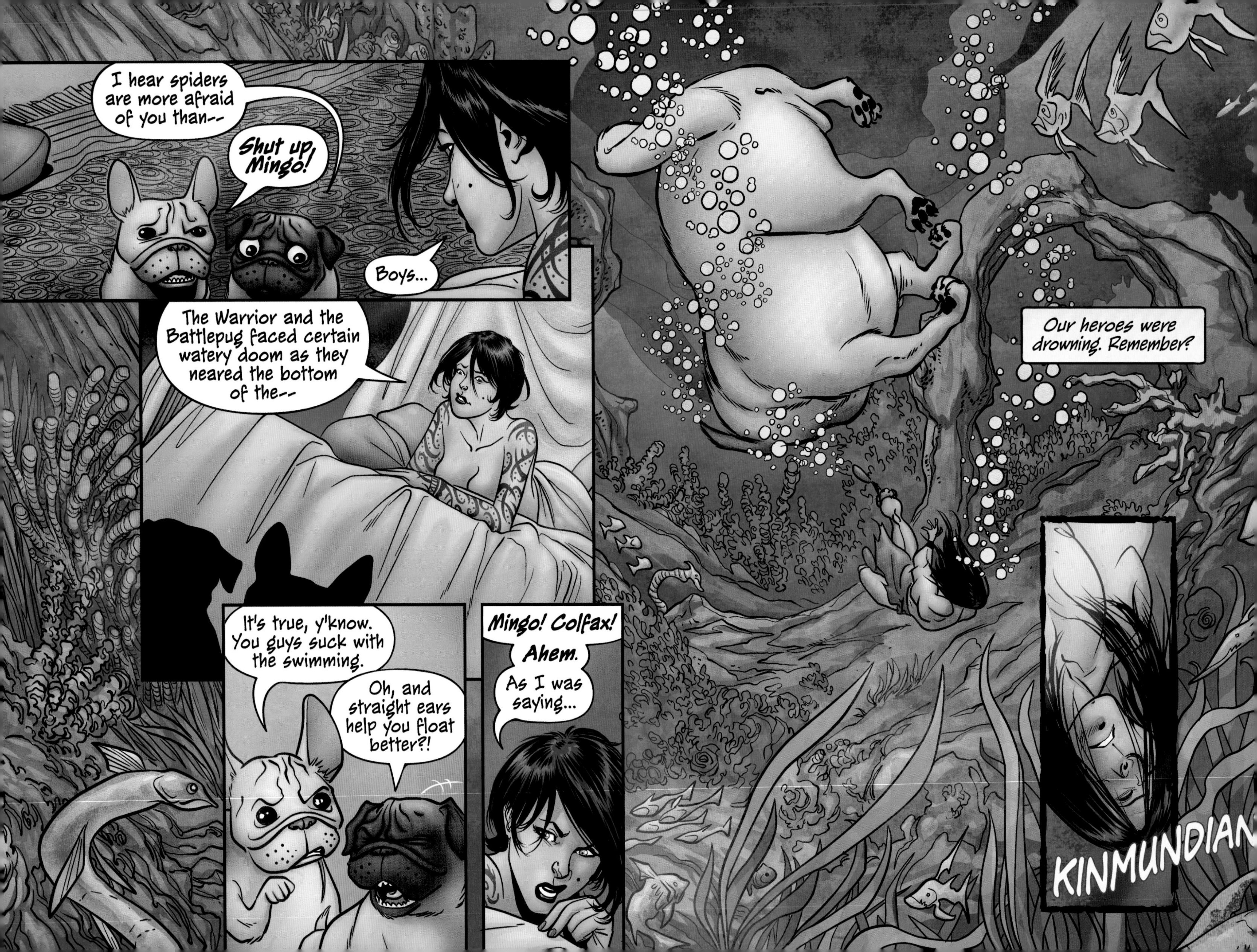
I hear spiders are more afraid of you than--
Shut up, Mingo!
Boys...
The Warrior and the Battlepug faced certain watery doom as they neared the bottom of the--
It's true, y'know. You guys suck with the swimming.
Oh, and straight ears help you float better?!
Mingo! Colfax!
Ahem.
As I was saying...
Our heroes were drowning. Remember?
KINMUNDIAN

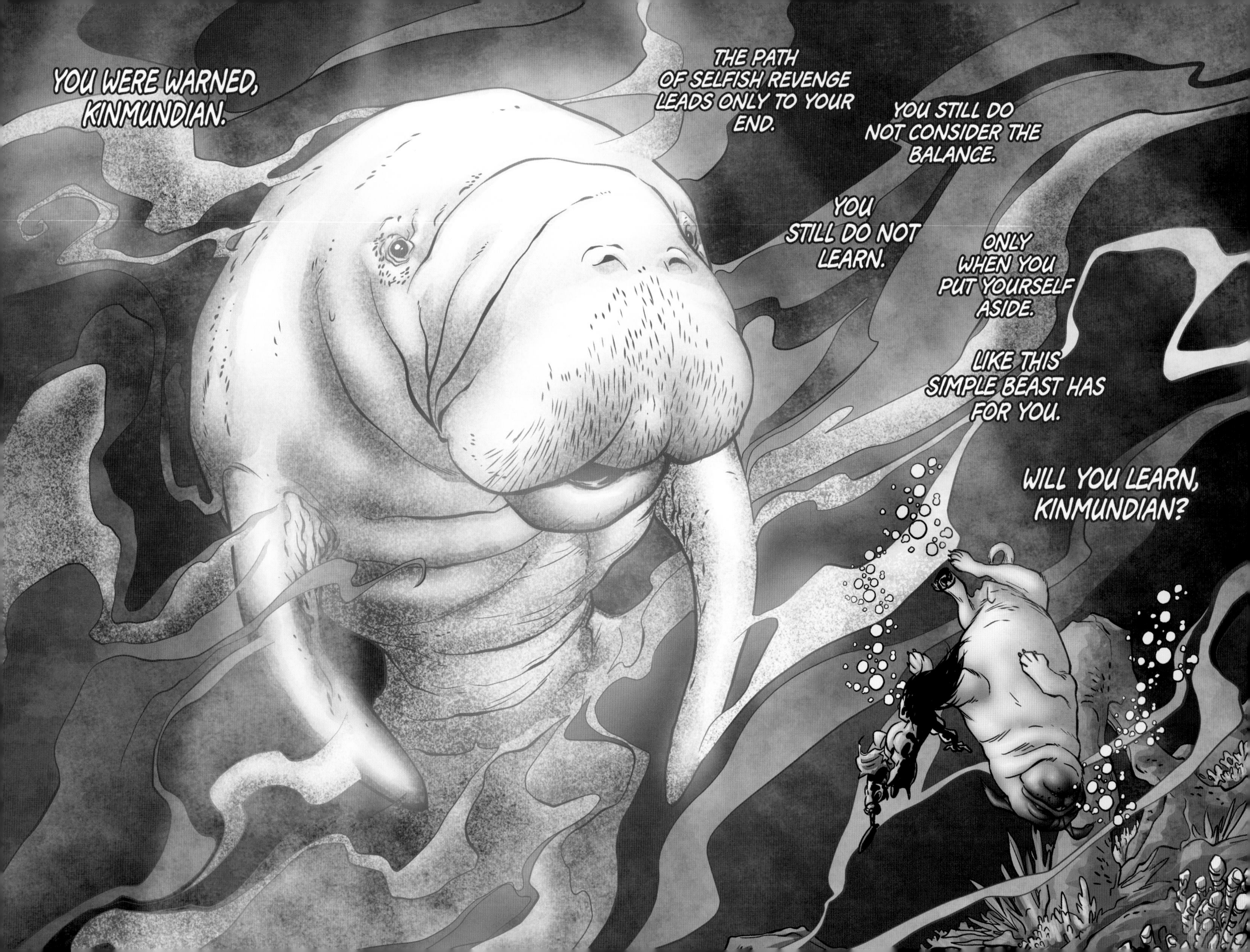
YOU WERE WARNED, KINMUNDIAN.
THE PATH OF SELFISH REVENGE LEADS ONLY TO YOUR END.
YOU STILL DO NOT CONSIDER THE BALANCE.
YOU STILL DO NOT LEARN.
ONLY WHEN YOU PUT YOURSELF ASIDE.
LIKE THIS SIMPLE BEAST HAS FOR YOU.
WILL YOU LEARN, KINMUNDIAN?

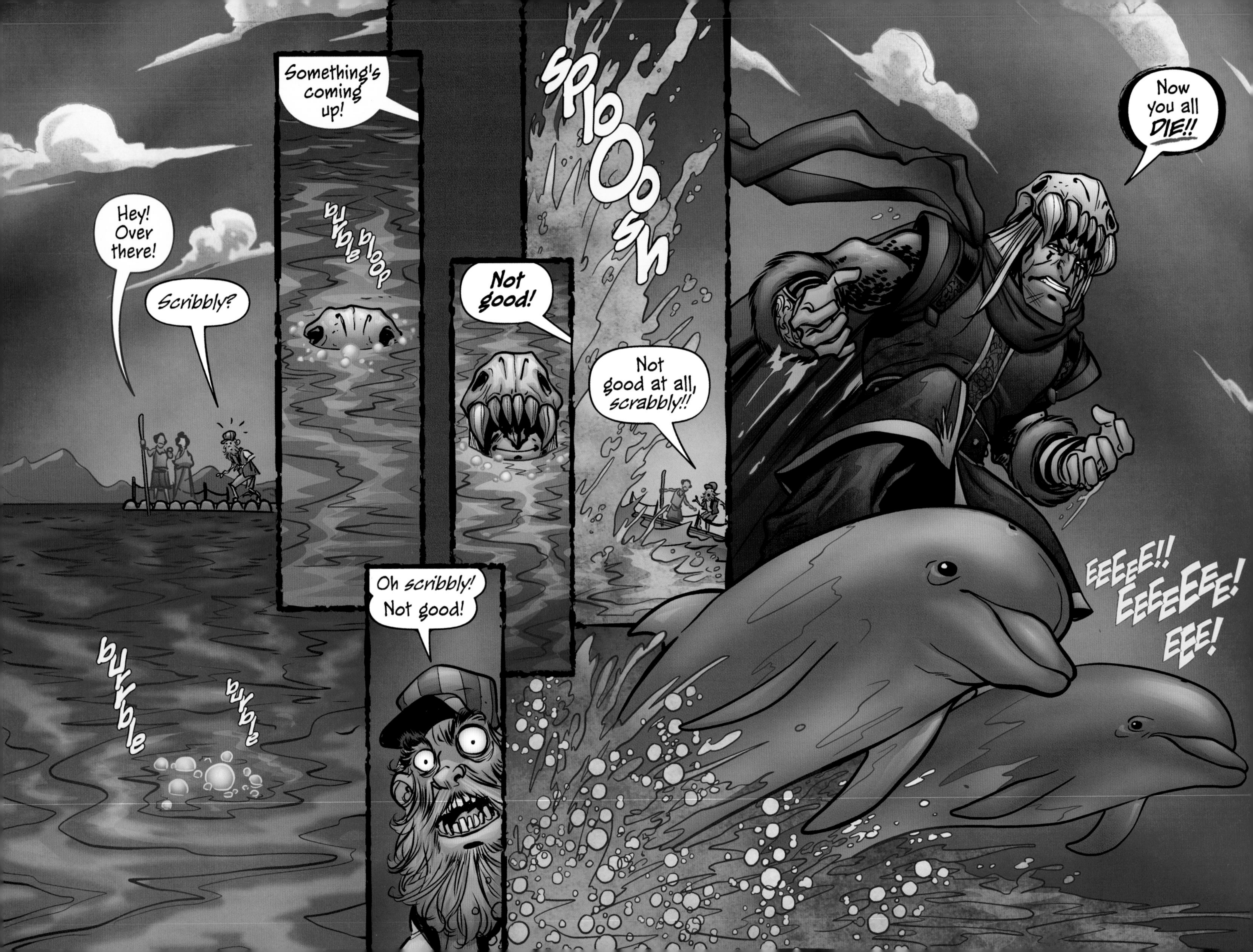
Hey! Over there!
Scribbly?
Something's coming up!
bubble bloop
Not good!
Not good at all, scrabbly!!
SPLOOOSH
Oh scribbly! Not good!
bubble
bubble
Now you all DIE!!
EEEEE!! EEEEEEE! EEE!

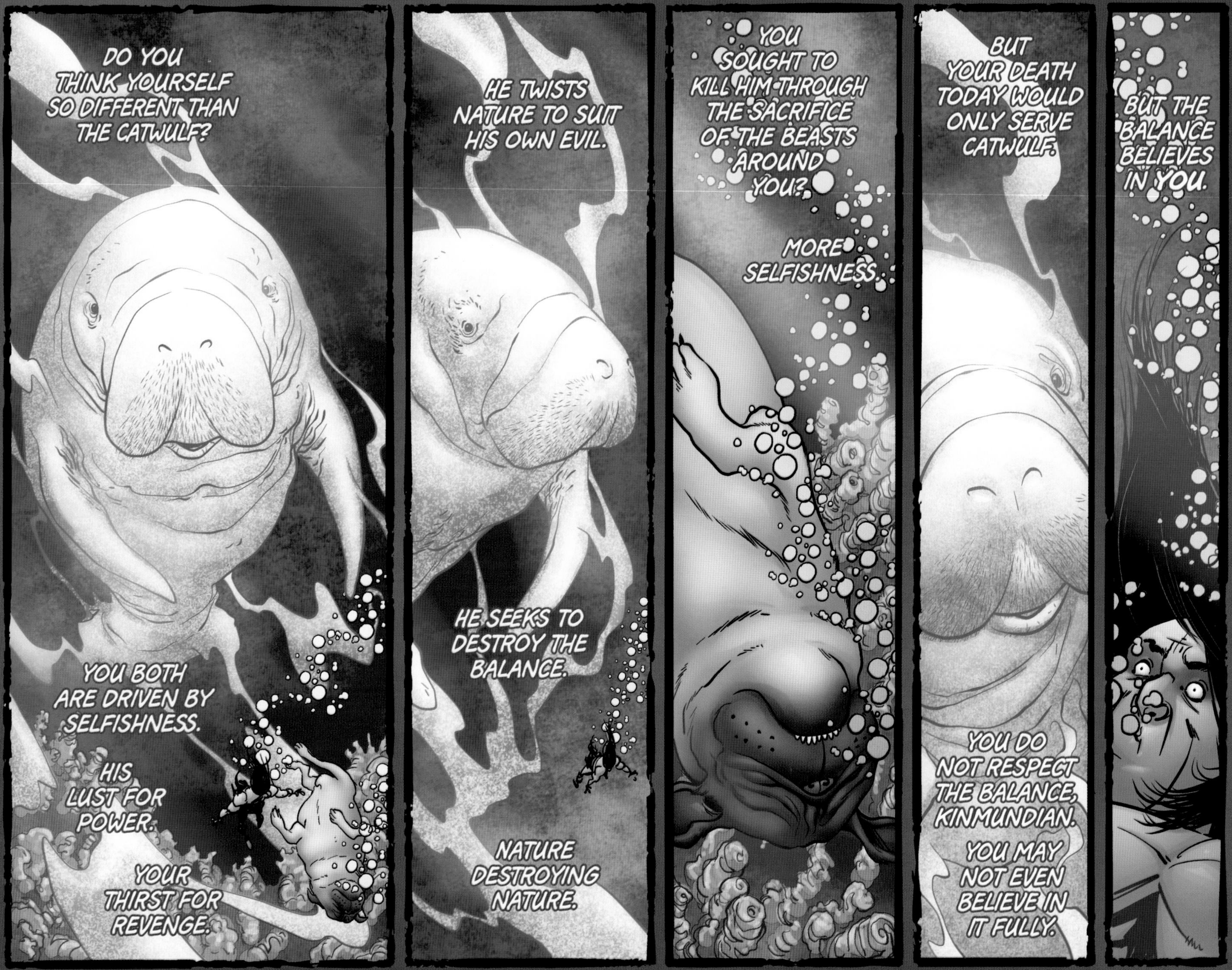
DO YOU THINK YOURSELF SO DIFFERENT THAN THE CATWULF?
YOU BOTH ARE DRIVEN BY SELFISHNESS.
HIS LUST FOR POWER.
YOUR THIRST FOR REVENGE.
HE TWISTS NATURE TO SUIT HIS OWN EVIL.
HE SEEKS TO DESTROY THE BALANCE.
NATURE DESTROYING NATURE.
YOU SOUGHT TO KILL HIM THROUGH THE SACRIFICE OF THE BEASTS AROUND YOU?
MORE SELFISHNESS.
BUT YOUR DEATH TODAY WOULD ONLY SERVE CATWULF.
YOU DO NOT RESPECT THE BALANCE, KINMUNDIAN.
YOU MAY NOT EVEN BELIEVE IN IT FULLY.
BUT THE BALANCE BELIEVES IN YOU.

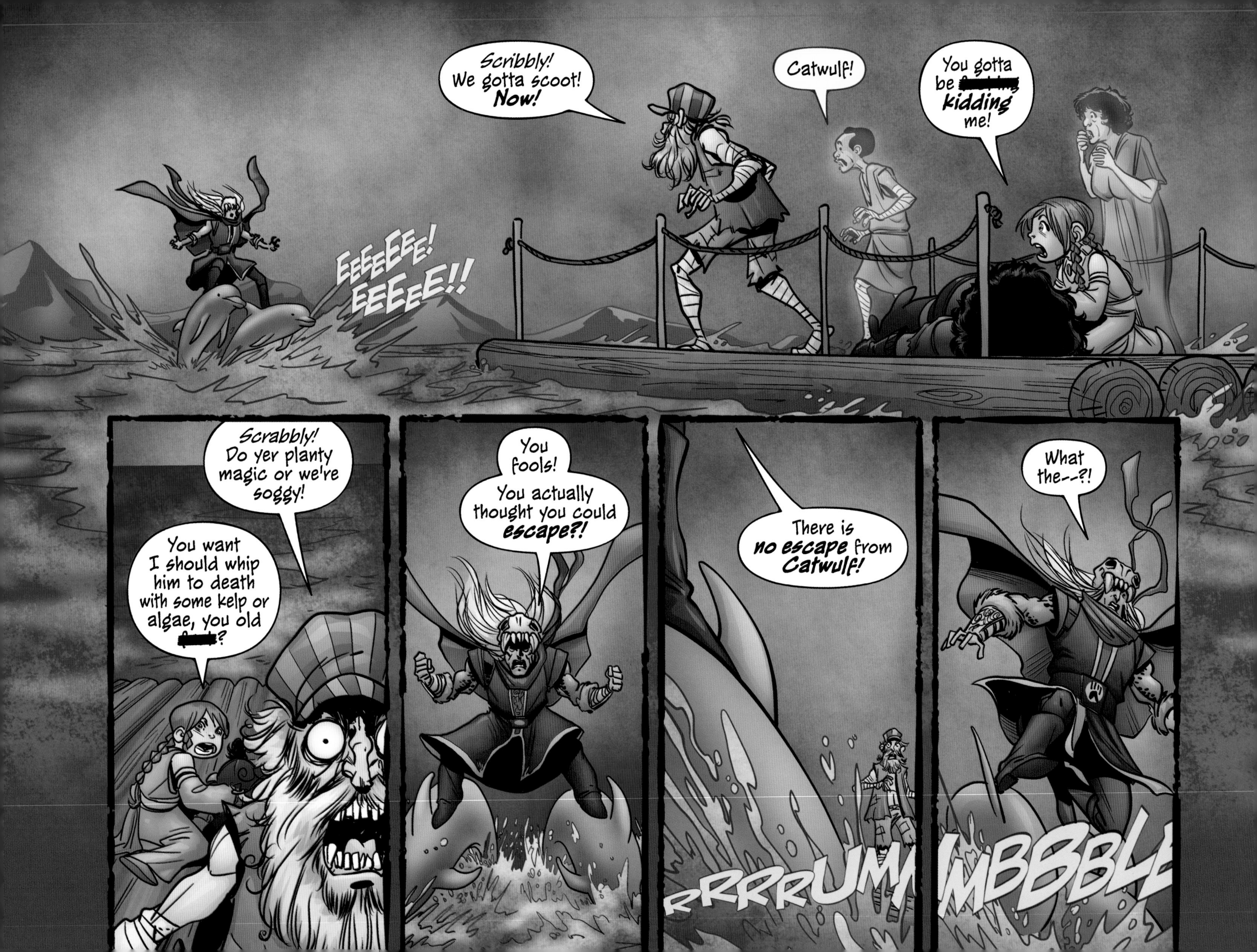
Scribbly! We gotta scoot! **Now!**
Catwulf!
You gotta be [redacted] **kidding** me!
EEEEEEE! EEEEE!!
Scrabbly! Do yer planty magic or we're soggy!
You want I should whip him to death with some kelp or algae, you old [redacted]?
You fools! You actually thought you could **escape?!**
There is **no escape** from **Catwulf!**
What the--?!
RRRRRUMMMBBBLE

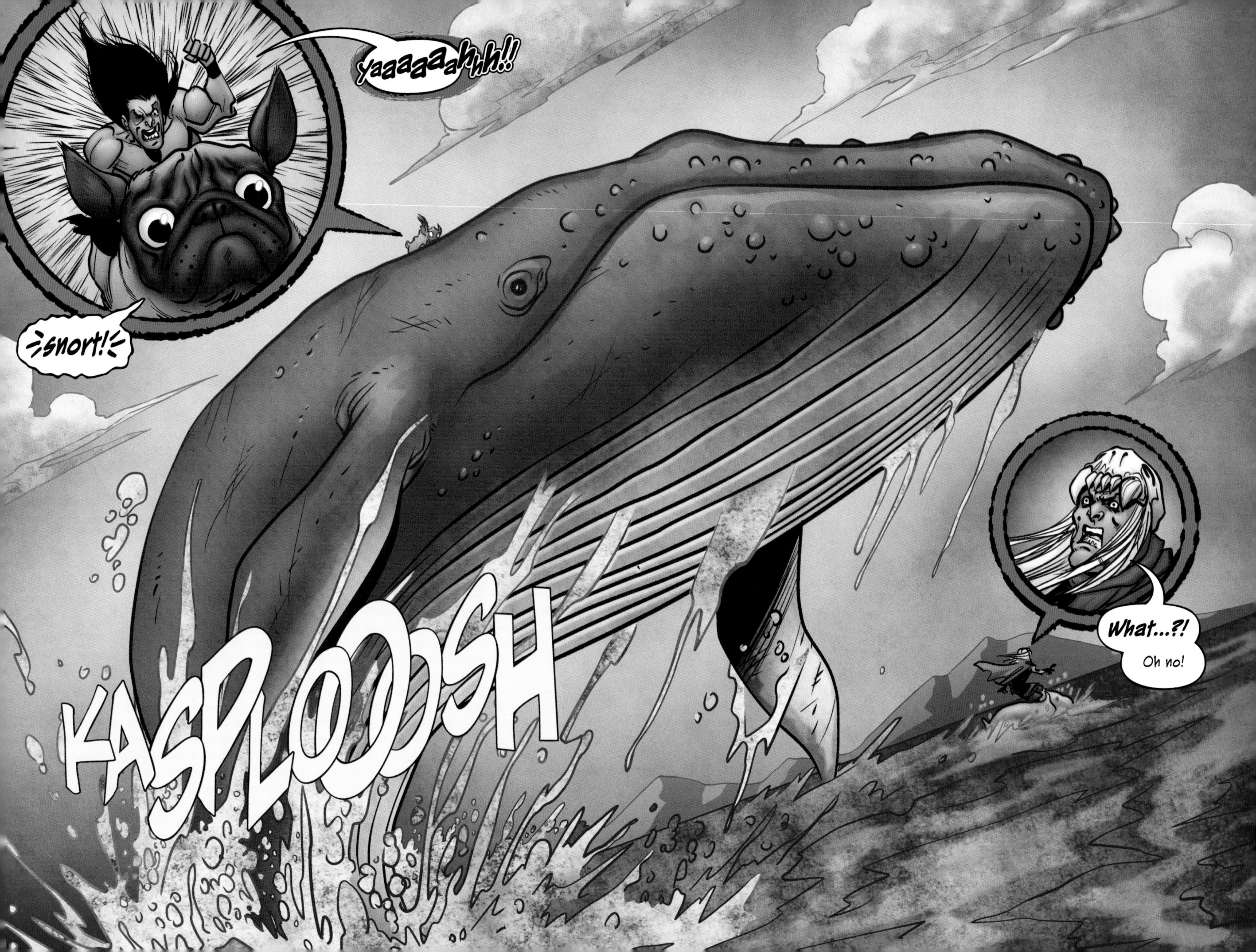
yaaaaaaahhh!!
snort!
KASPLOOOSH
What...?!
Oh no!

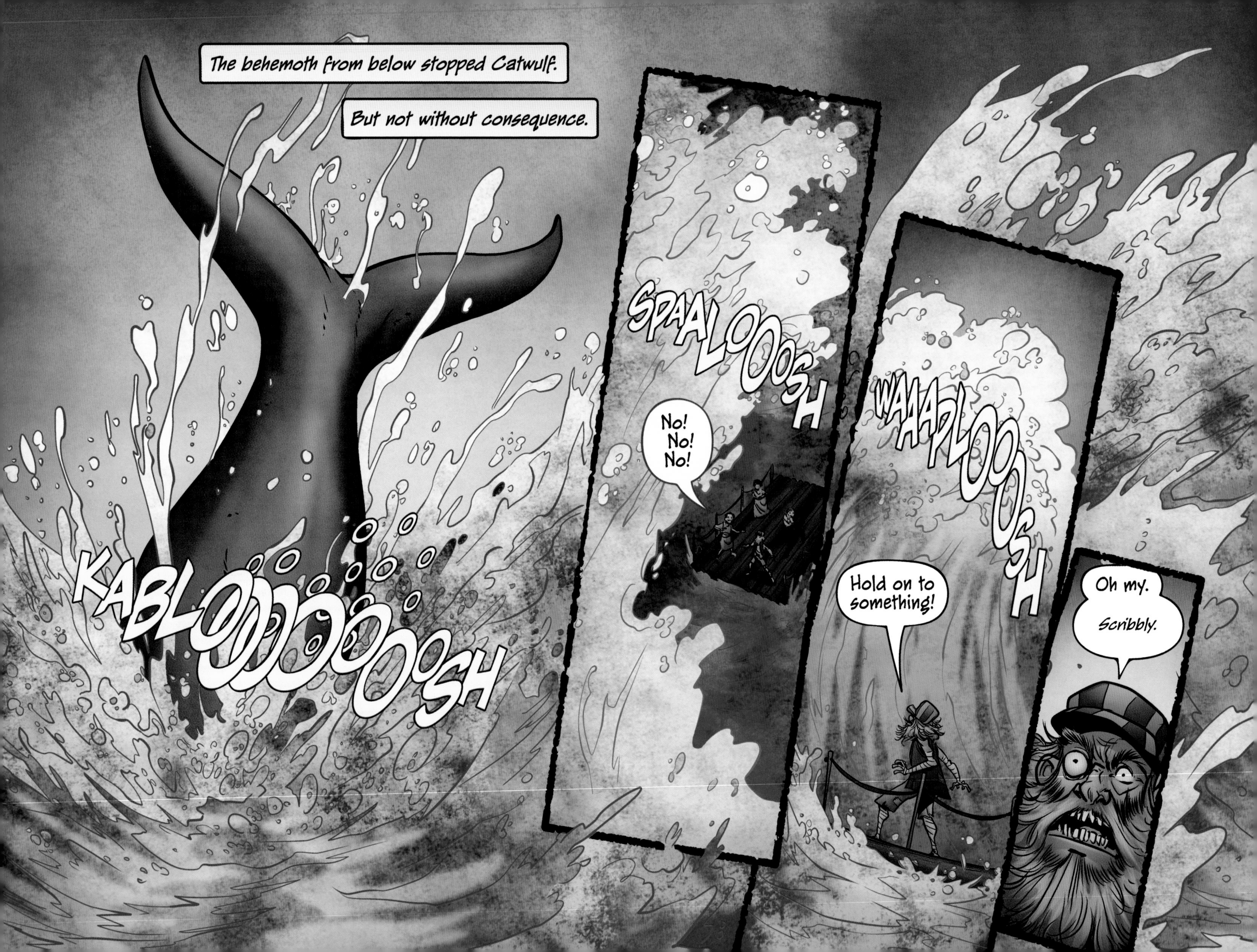
The behemoth from below stopped Catwulf.
But not without consequence.
KABLOOOOOOOSH
SPAALOOOSH
No! No! No!
WAAAPLOOOSH
Hold on to something!
Oh my.
Scribbly.

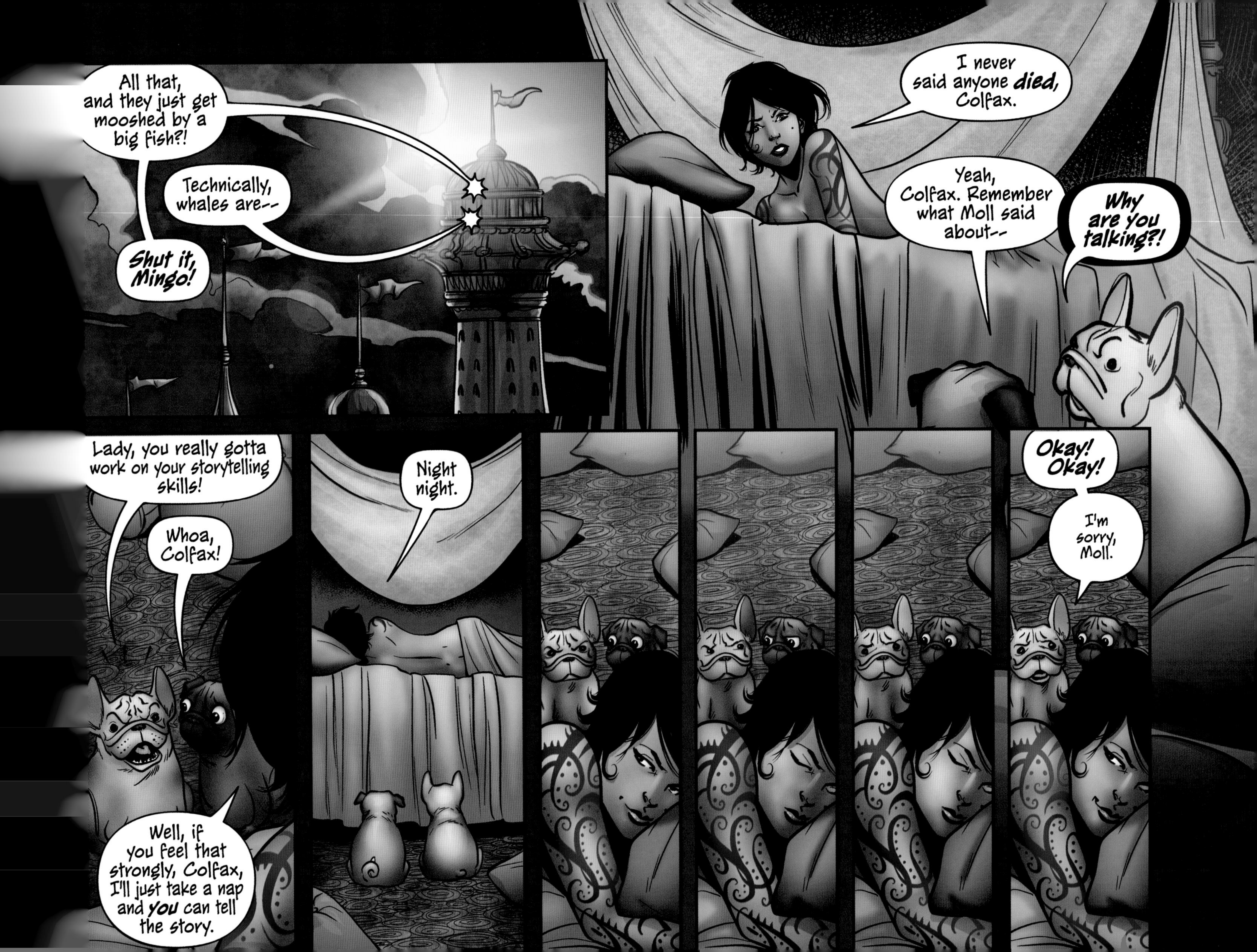
All that, and they just get mooshed by a big fish?!
Technically, whales are--
Shut it, Mingo!
I never said anyone died, Colfax.
Yeah, Colfax. Remember what Moll said about--
Why are you talking?!
Lady, you really gotta work on your storytelling skills!
Whoa, Colfax!
Well, if you feel that strongly, Colfax, I'll just take a nap and you can tell the story.
Night night.
Okay! Okay!
I'm sorry, Moll.

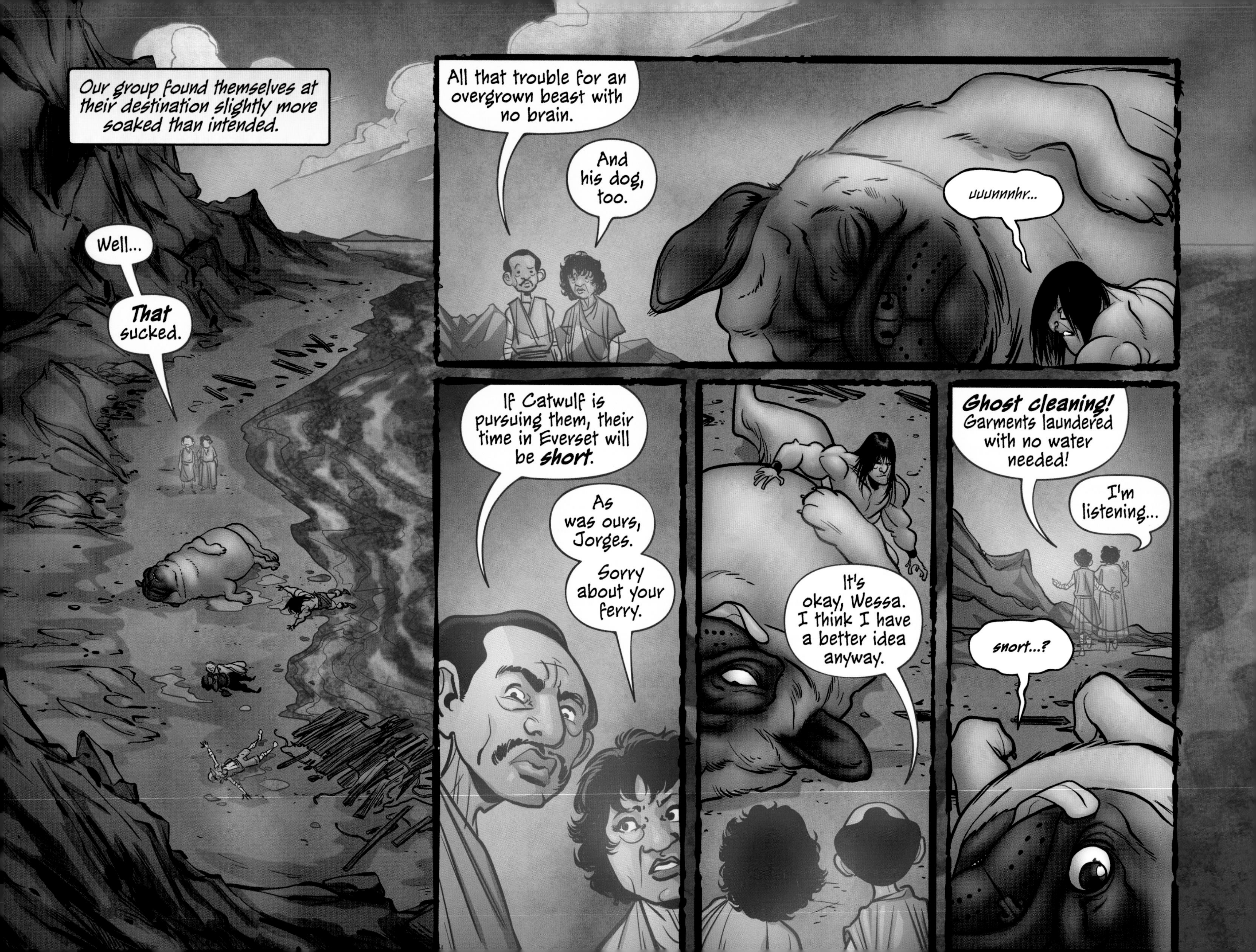
Our group found themselves at their destination slightly more soaked than intended.
Well...
That sucked.
All that trouble for an overgrown beast with no brain.
And his dog, too.
uuunnnhr...
If Catwulf is pursuing them, their time in Everset will be short.
As was ours, Jorges.
Sorry about your ferry.
It's okay, Wessa. I think I have a better idea anyway.
Ghost cleaning! Garments laundered with no water needed!
I'm listening...
snort...?

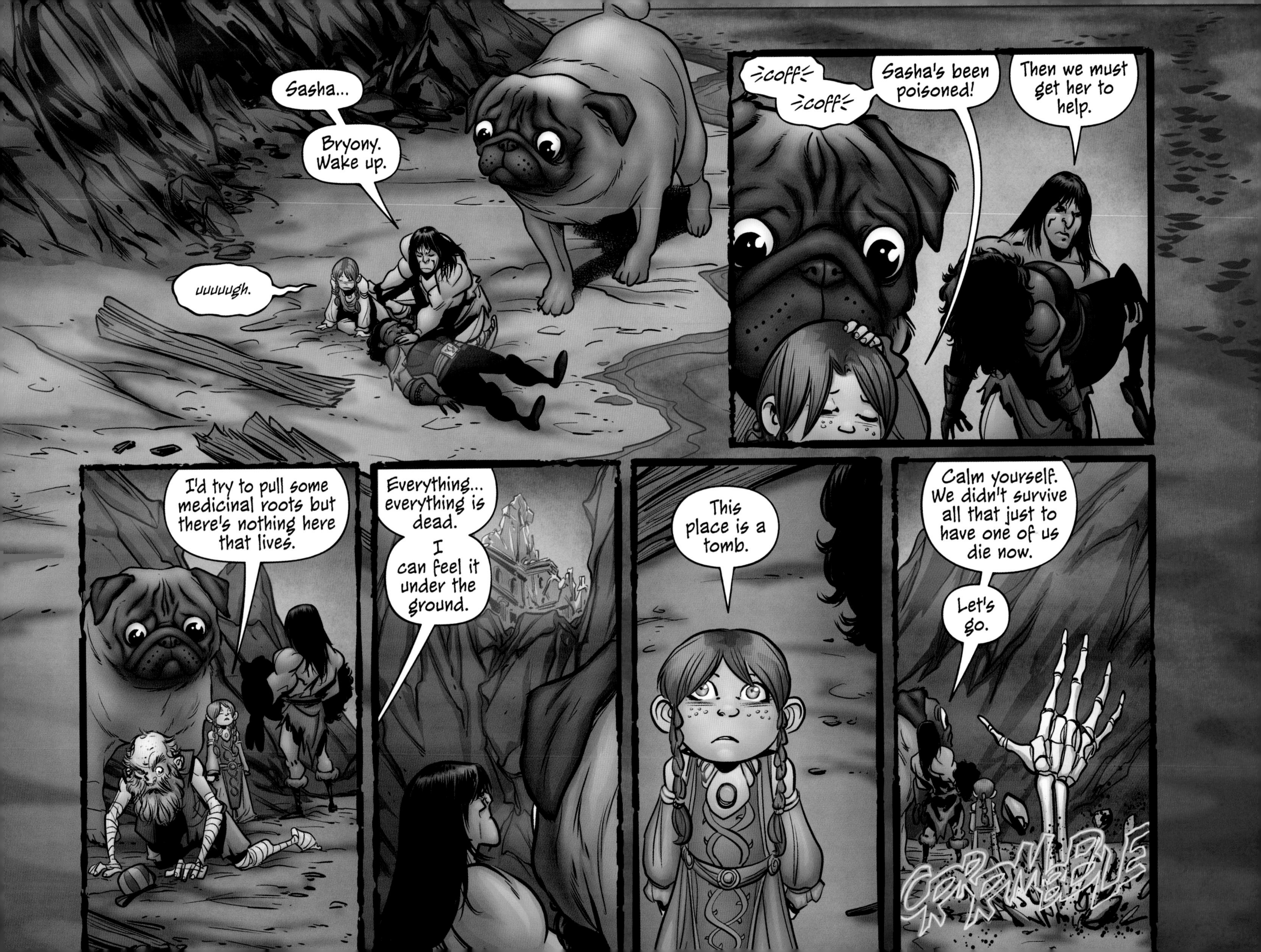

Sasha...
Bryony. Wake up.
uuuuugh.
coff
coff
Sasha's been poisoned!
Then we must get her to help.
I'd try to pull some medicinal roots but there's nothing here that lives.
Everything... everything is dead.
I can feel it under the ground.
This place is a tomb.
Calm yourself. We didn't survive all that just to have one of us die now.
Let's go.
SCRAMBLE

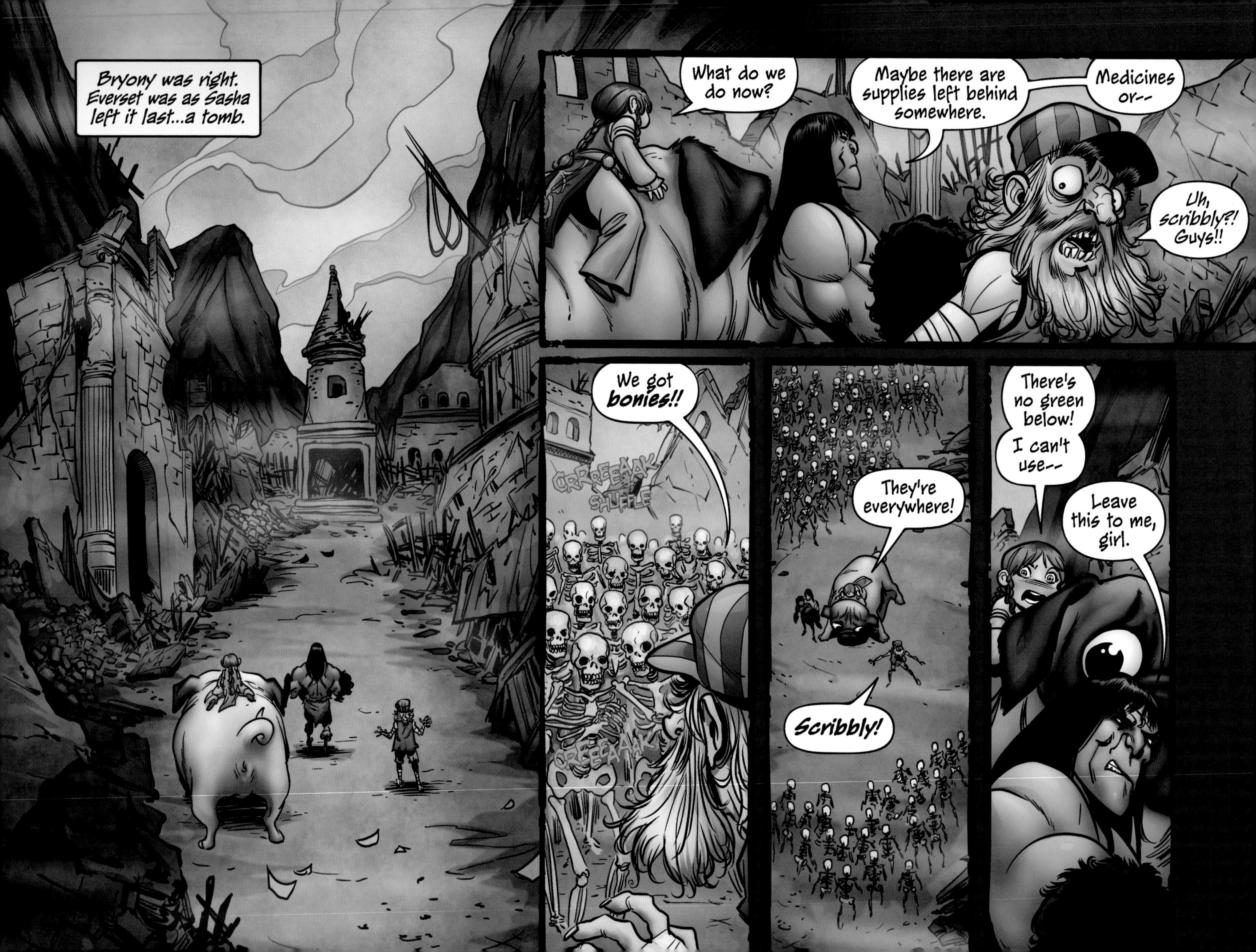

Bryony was right. Everset was as Sasha left it last...a tomb.
What do we do now?
Maybe there are supplies left behind somewhere.
Medicines or--
Uh, scribbly?! Guys!!
We got **bonies!!**
CRRREEAAK
SHUFFLE
CRREEAAAK
They're everywhere!
Scribbly!
There's no green below!
I can't use--
Leave this to me, girl.

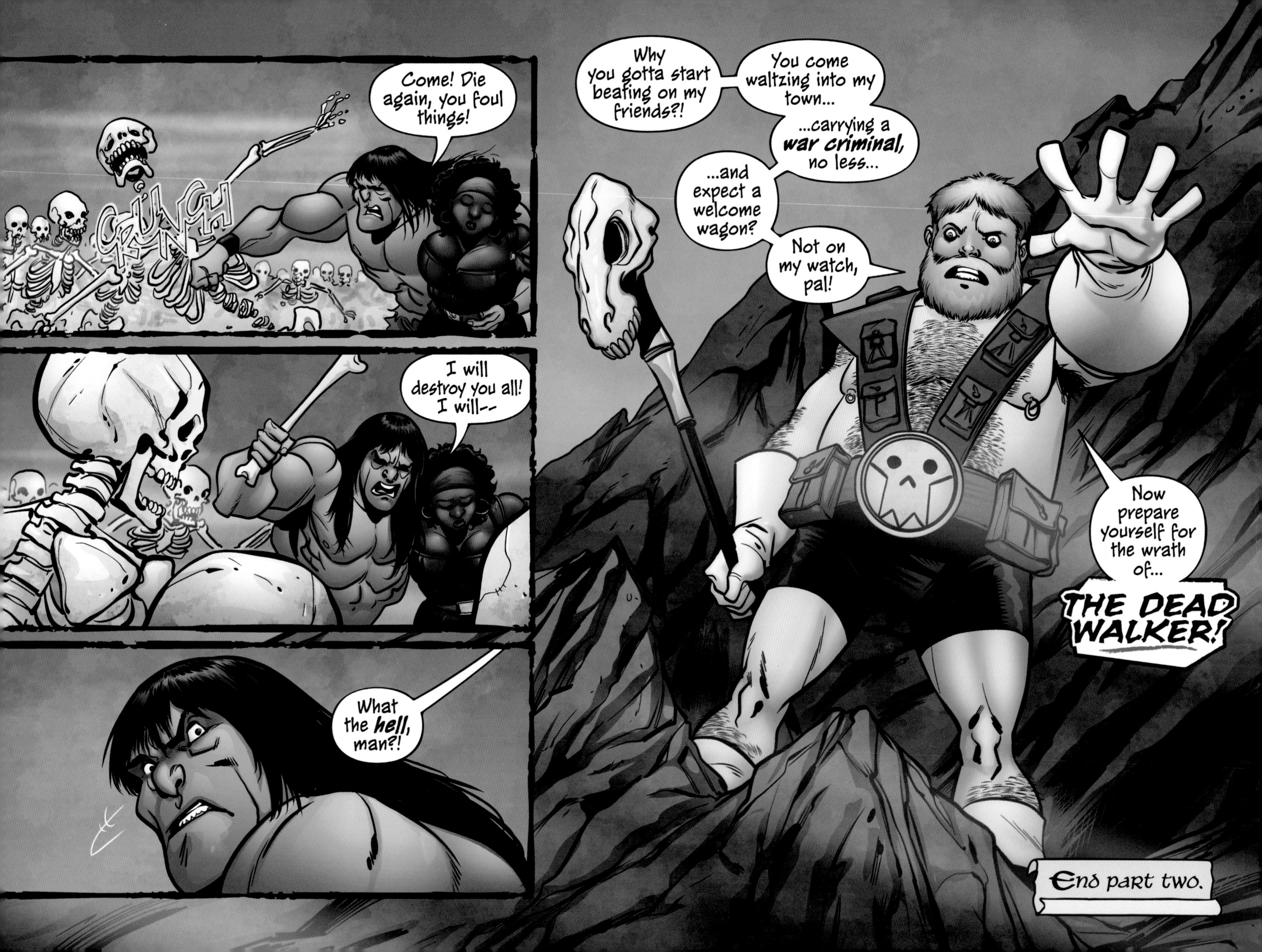
Come! Die again, you foul things!
CRUNCH
CRUNCH
I will destroy you all! I will--
What the *hell*, man?!
Why you gotta start beating on my friends?!
You come waltzing into my town...
...carrying a ***war criminal***, no less...
...and expect a welcome wagon?
Not on my watch, pal!
Now prepare yourself for the wrath of...
THE DEAD WALKER!
End part two.

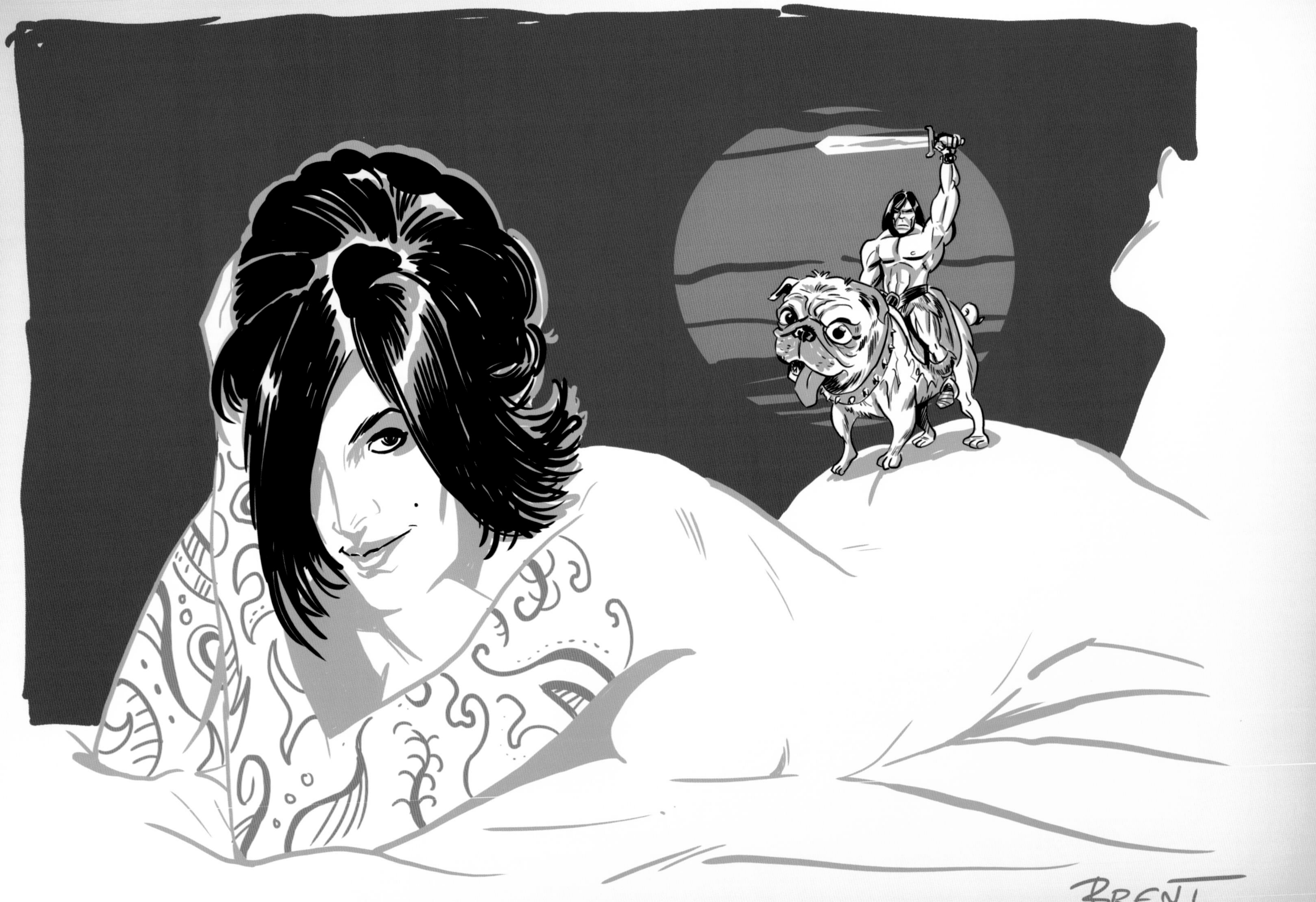
BRENT

Brent Schoonover

Chris Brunner

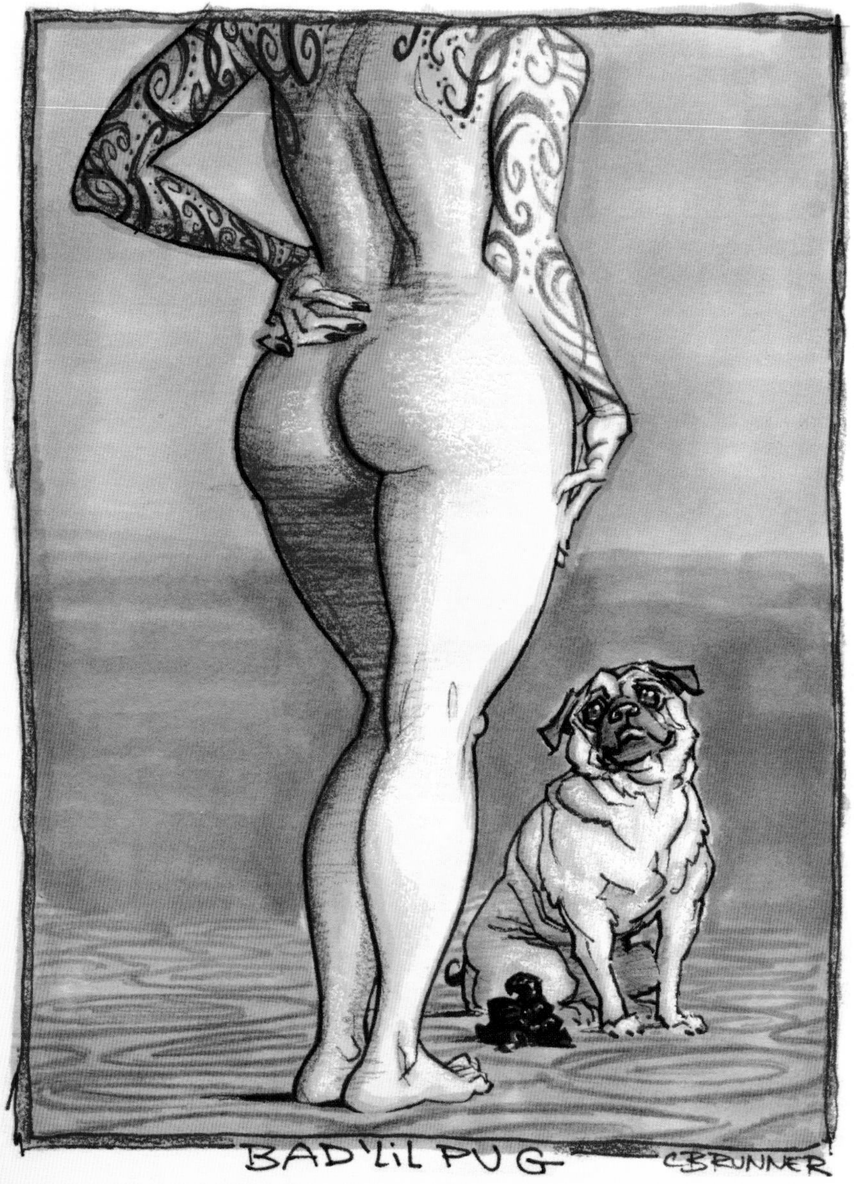
BAD'LiL PUG
CBRUNNER

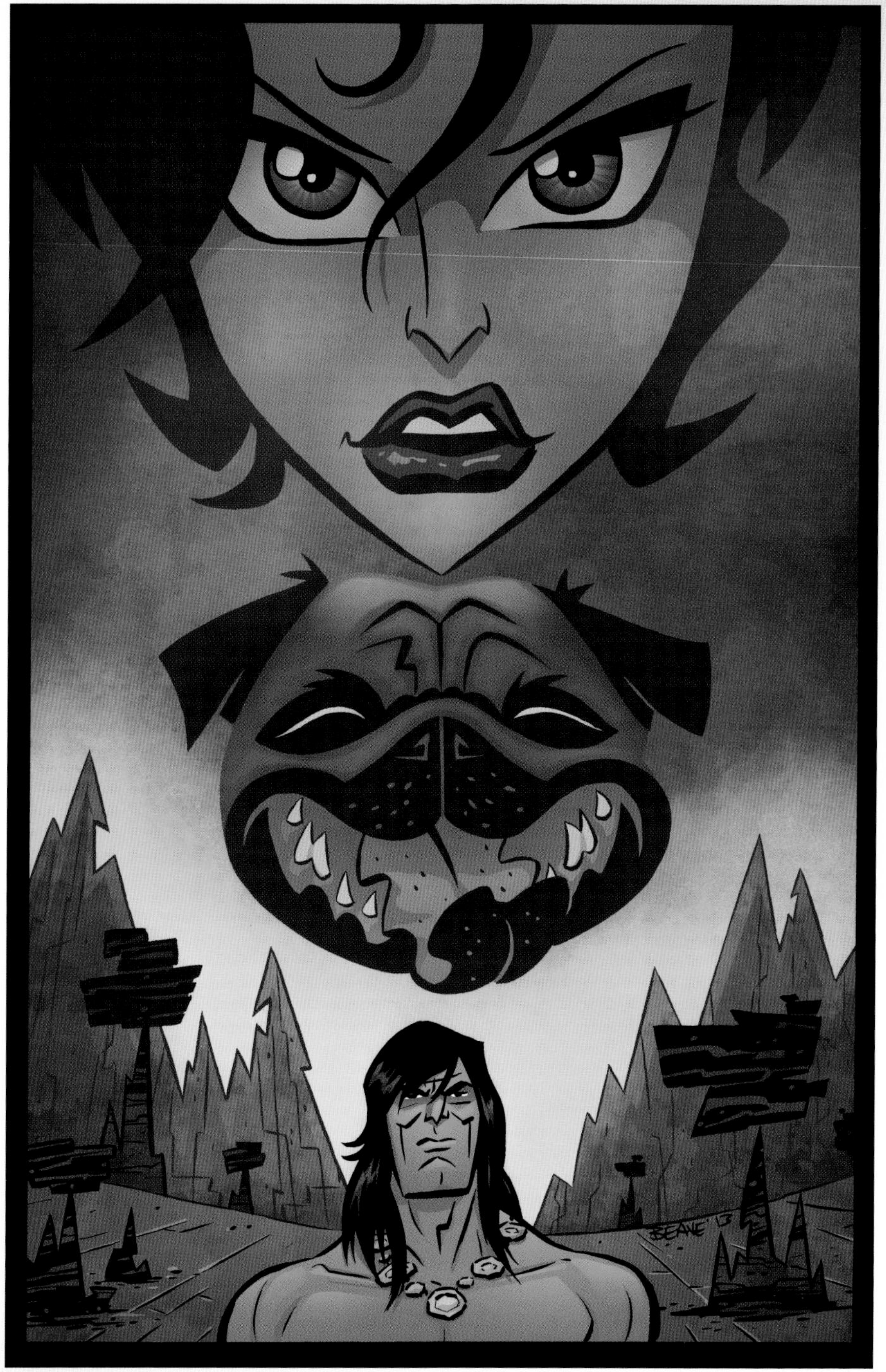
BEAVE '13

Ethen Beavers

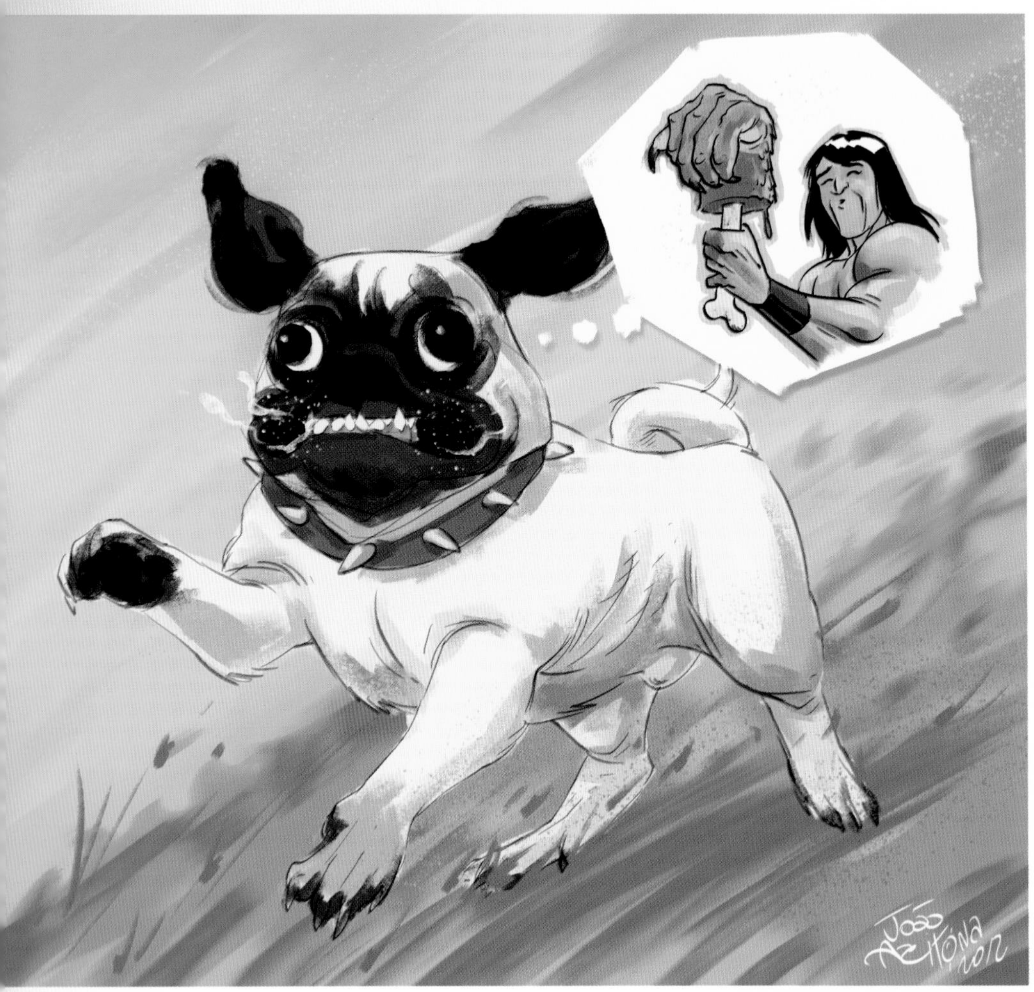

João Vieira

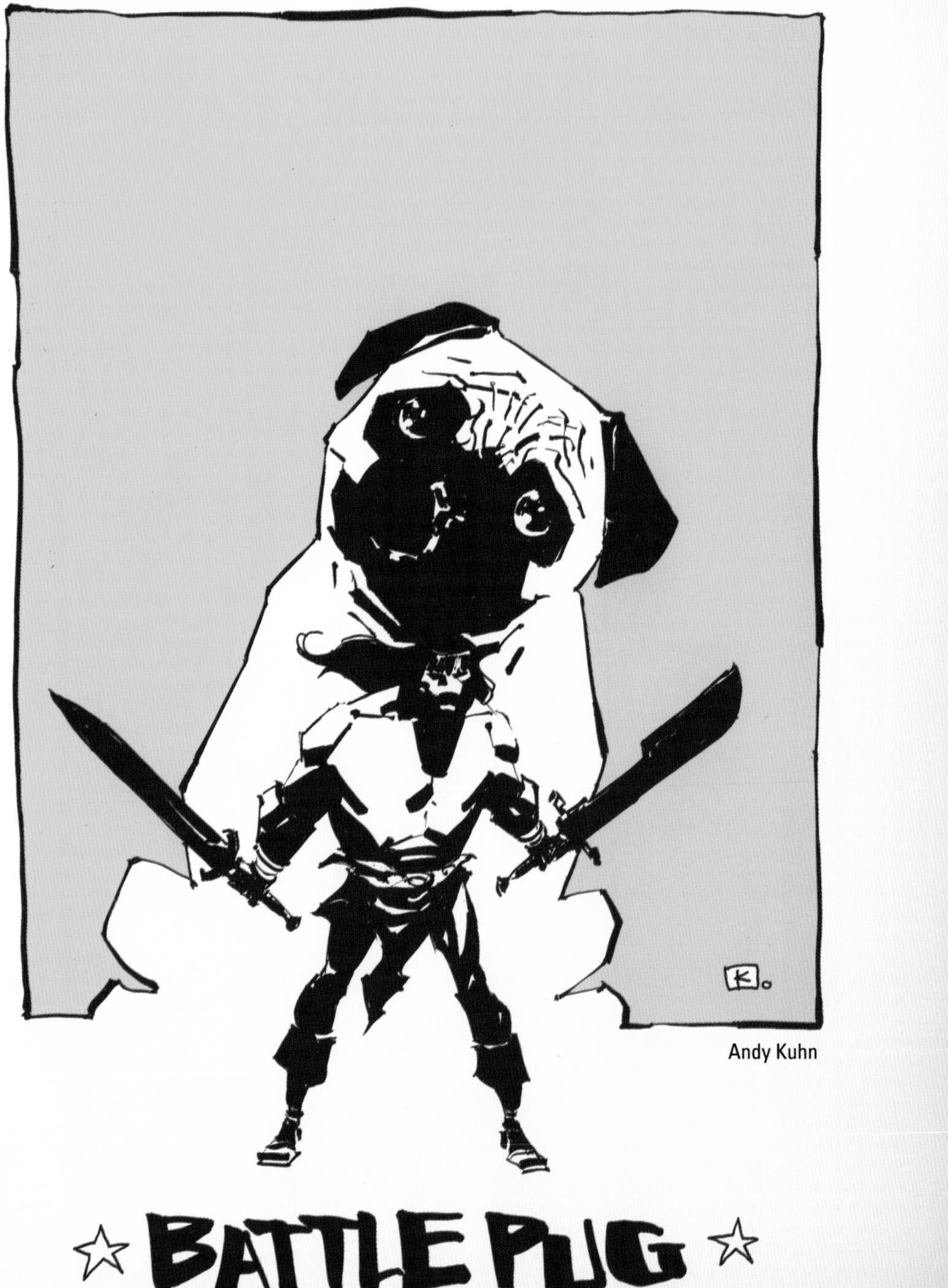
☆ BATTLE PUG ☆

Andy Kuhn

Greg Titus

Emily Stone

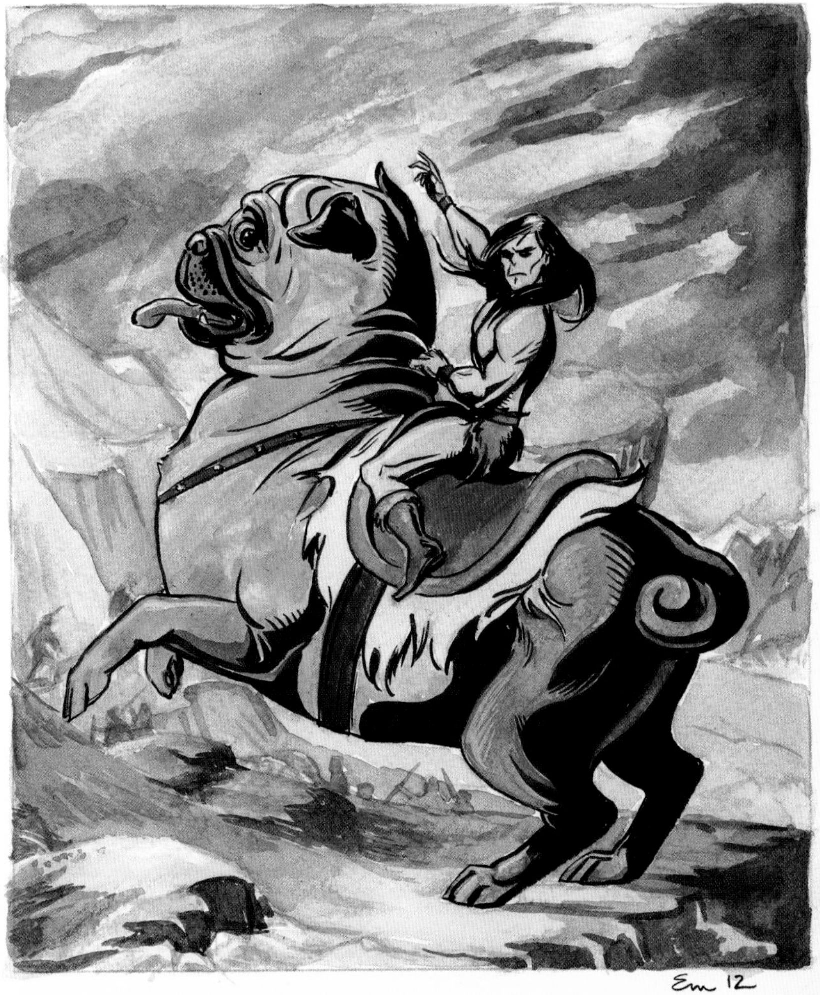

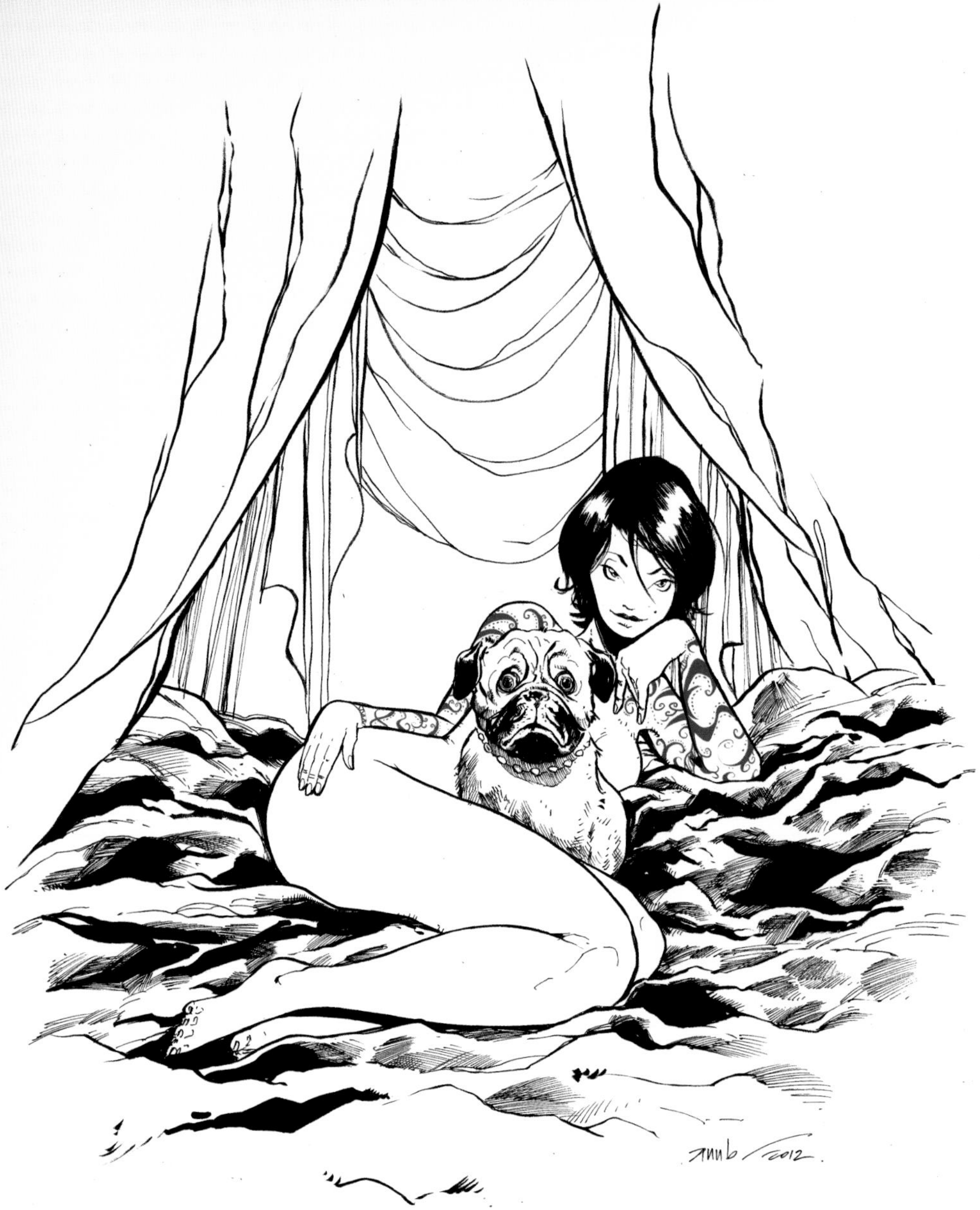

Amancay Nahuelpan

CREATOR BIOGRAPHIES

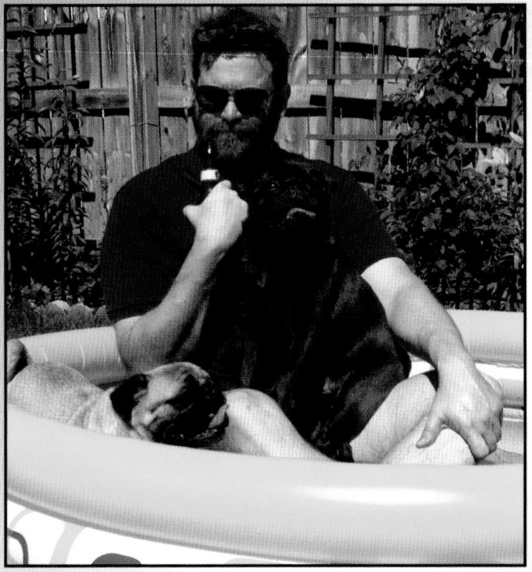

MIKE NORTON

Mike Norton has been working in comics for over ten years, gaining recognition for projects such as *The Waiting Place* and *Jason and the Argobots*. He's made a name for himself working on books like *Queen and Country*, *Gravity*, *Runaways*, *The All New Atom*, *Green Arrow/Black Canary*, *Billy Batson and the Magic of Shazam!*, and *Young Justice*. He is currently drawing Marvel's *Fear Itself: Youth in Revolt*, and his own weekly webcomic, *Battlepug*. He is also very, very tall.

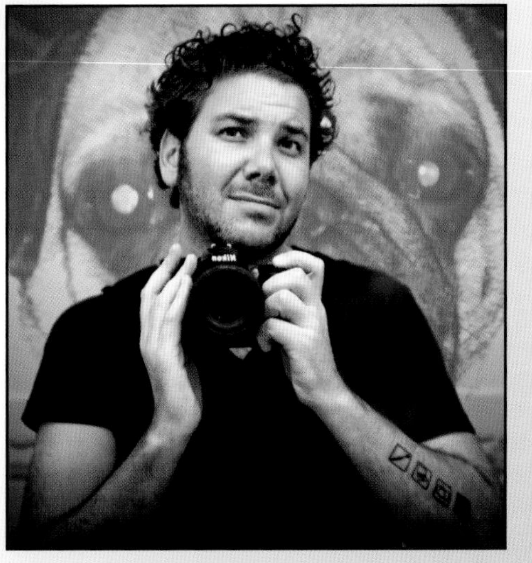

ALLEN PASSALAQUA

Allen is a professional comic color artist, as well as being involved in promoting culture and art and bringing together the creative community. Combining traditional and pop-culture influences, Allen has been commissioned to create artwork for several national parks, the San Diego Zoo, and the Grand Canyon, has story boarded Emmy-winning commercials, and has worked on various mass-media-outlet projects. His coloring work includes *Justice Society of America*, *Spider-Man*, *Green Arrow/Black Canary*, *Detective Comics*, and many others. He is not as tall as Mike.

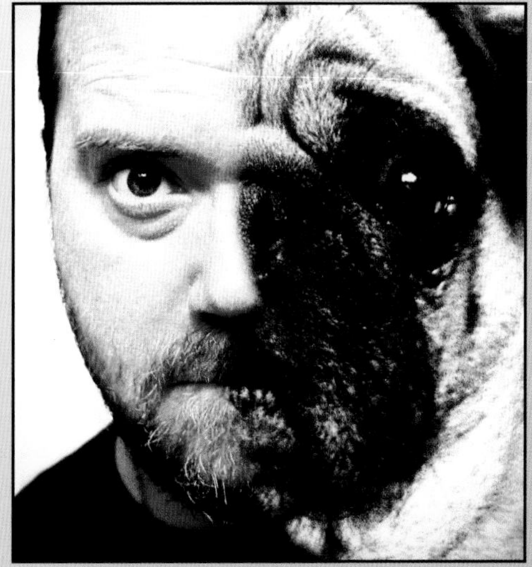

CHRIS CRANK

The letterer, musician, and editing pal Crank is believed to be a myth, and he must let the world think that he is a myth, until he can find a way to control the snotty spirit that dwells within him. Crank once baby-sat Mike's first pug for a whole weekend without damaging him, and he has a podcast with Mike at CrankCast.net.

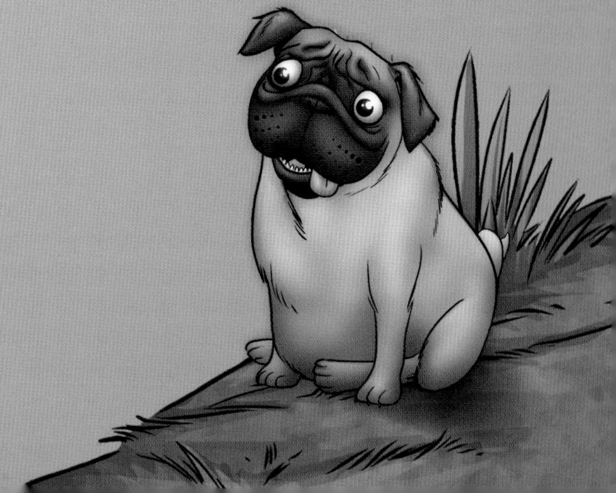

DARK HORSE BRINGS YOU THE BEST IN WEBCOMICS!

COLLECT ALL OF YOUR FAVORITE ONLINE SENSATIONS, NOW IN PRINT WITH LOADS OF AWESOME EXTRAS NOT FOUND ANYWHERE ELSE!

ACHEWOOD
By Chris Onstad

Since 2001, cult comic favorite *Achewood* has built a six-figure international following. Intelligent, hilarious, and adult but not filthy, it's the strip you'll wish you'd discovered as an underappreciated fifteen-year-old. "I'm addicted to *Achewood*. Chris Onstad is a dark, hilarious genius." –Dave Barry

Volume 1: The Great Outdoor Fight HC
ISBN 978-1-59307-997-0 | $14.99

Volume 2: Worst Song, Played on Ugliest Guitar HC
ISBN 978-1-59582-239-0 | $15.99

Volume 3: A Home for Scared People HC
ISBN 978-1-59582-450-9 | $16.99

AXE COP
By Malachai Nicolle and Ethan Nicolle

Created by five-year-old Malachai Nicolle and illustrated by his older brother, the cartoonist Ethan Nicolle, these *Axe Cop* volumes collect the hit webcomic that has captured the world's attention with its insanely imaginative adventures, as well as the *Axe Cop* print-only adventures. Whether he's fighting gun-toting dinosaurs, teaming up with Ninja Moon Warriors, or answering readers' questions via his insightful advice column, "Ask Axe Cop," the adventures of Axe Cop and his incomparable team of crime fighters will delight and perplex even the most stoic of readers.

Volume 1
ISBN 978-1-59582-681-7 | $14.99

Volume 2: Bad Guy Earth
ISBN 978-1-59582-825-5 | $12.99

Volume 3
ISBN 978-1-59582-911-5 | $14.99

Volume 4: President of the World
ISBN 978-1-61655-057-8 | $12.99

PENNY ARCADE
By Jerry Holkins and Mike Krahulik

Penny Arcade, the comic strip for gamers, by gamers, is now available in comic shops and bookstores everywhere. Experience the joy of being a hardcore gamer as expressed in hilariously witty vignettes of random vulgarity and mindless violence!

Volume 1: Attack of the Bacon Robots! TPB
ISBN 978-1-59307-444-9 | $12.99

Volume 2: Epic Legends of the Magic Sword Kings TPB
ISBN 978-1-59307-541-5 | $12.99

Volume 3: The WarSun Prophecies TPB
ISBN 978-1-59307-635-1 | $12.99

Volume 4: Birds Are Weird TPB
ISBN 978-1-59307-773-0 | $12.99

Volume 5: The Case of the Mummy's Gold TPB
ISBN 978-1-59307-814-0 | $12.99

THE ADVENTURES OF DR. MCNINJA
By Christopher Hastings

He's a doctor! He's a ninja! Read about his mighty exploits! These books offer a hefty dose of science, action, and outrageous comedy. With haunted spaceships, sentient dinosaurs, and an evil unicorn motorcycle, it's more adventure than your puny mind can handle!

Night Powers
ISBN 978-1-59582-709-8 | $19.99

Timefist
ISBN 978-1-61655-069-1 | $19.99

Omnibus
ISBN 978-1-61655-112-4 | $24.99

WONDERMARK
By David Malki

Dark Horse Comics is proud to present these handsome hardbound collections of David Malki's Ignatz-nominated comic strip *Wondermark*. Malki repurposes illustrations and engravings from nineteenth century books into hilarious, collage-style comic strips. More than just webcomic collections, the *Wondermark* books have been praised for their magnificent design and loads of extra content for casual readers and superfans alike.

Volume 1: Beards of Our Forefathers HC
ISBN 978-1-59307-984-0 | $14.99

Volume 2: Clever Tricks to Stave Off Death HC
ISBN 978-1-59582-329-8 | $14.99

Volume 3: Dapper Caps & Pedal-Copters HC
ISBN 978-1-59582-449-3 | $16.99

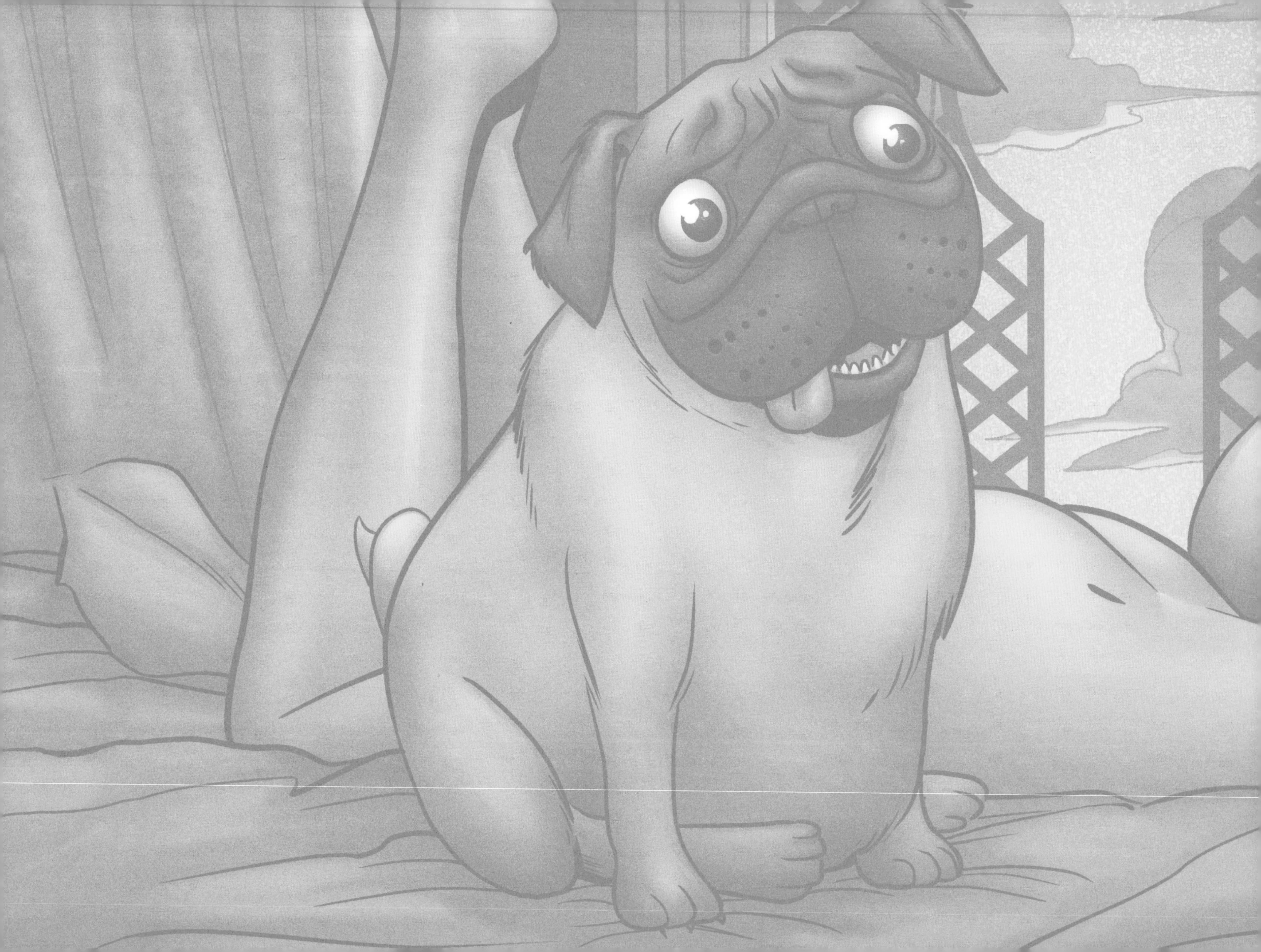